Secondary English
and Literacy

Secondary English and Literacy

A Guide for Teachers

AVRIL HAWORTH,
CHRISTOPHER TURNER AND
MARGARET WHITELEY

P·C·P

Paul Chapman
Publishing

Paul Chapman Publishing
A SAGE Publications Company
1 Olivers Yard
London EC1Y 1SP

SAGE Publications Inc
2455 Teller Road
Thousand Oaks, California 91320

SAGE Publications India Pvt Ltd
B-42, Panchsheel Enclave
Post Box 4109
New Delhi 100 017

Library of Congress Control Number: available

A catalogue record for this book is available from the British Library

ISBN 0-7619-4280-7
ISBN 0-7619- 4281-5 (pbk)

Typeset by Dorwyn Ltd, Rowlands Castle, Hants
Printed in Great Britain by Athenaeum Press, Gateshead

Contents

Acknowledgements   vi

Preface   vii

Glossary of Terms   xiii

1   Introduction: English and Literacy   1

2   Language Study   12

3   Investigating Grammar   35

4   Writing   49

5   Reading and Literature   65

6   Oracy in English   90

7   Drama in English   102

8   Media in English   123

9   ICT in English   139

10   The Future of English   155

Appendices   161

Bibliography   171

Index   175

This book is dedicated to all the trainee teachers of English we have worked with. We wish to recognize their contributions to the development of the thinking reflected in this book.

Acknowledgements

The authors and publishers would like to thank Hodder & Stoughton for permission to reprint the LINC Diagram from *Knowledge about Language and the National Curriculum* by Ronald Carter, Hodder and Stoughton, 1990.

Preface

One of the first principles of writing is to remember the readership – know who is going to read the text, and write with them in mind. The problem here, however, is that there could well be a diverse readership for this book. What unites you all is that you want to be teachers in secondary schools and colleges specializing in the teaching of English/Literacy.

The writers of the book are well aware that some of you are following a traditional one-year, full-time postgraduate course. However, we also know that some of you will be training to become teachers in a variety of other ways, including school-based, part-time and distance learning routes. You are all very welcome!

The variety of routes is testimony to the UK government's desire to make becoming a teacher as flexible as it can be, to cater for the range of factors that have impeded some people in the past.

That does not mean, however, that the process ought to be less rigorous or demanding. Indeed, one of the principles that has exercised the writers of this book has been a desire to provide potential English/Literacy teachers with an intellectually challenging framework for both the subject and its associated pedagogy. Expect to have to rethink, face new concepts and consider the implications for the classroom. We wish you well, with the book as well as with your training. We are all committed to preparing teachers who are going to be very good indeed; the pupils deserve the very best, and so does our subject. We hope that this volume contributes to the process.

HOW TO USE THE BOOK

Writing a book for multiple readerships is a challenge, and we want to reach a wide and diverse audience. We have tried very hard to make the book accessible and useful to all the likely readers. Given that range and variety, we set out to do the following with the book:

- write a companion text for those doing a one-year, full-time course – support and material in addition to that provided on your course

- provide trainee teachers on school-based and part-time courses with accessible support materials

- create an interactive workbook for those on distance learning courses.

With those aims in mind, you will notice that:

- the chapters cover the Attainment Targets for English

- the book addresses the key elements of the subject domain

- there are tasks, and pauses for thought – all designed to enable you to reflect on issues, to support the development of your pedagogic practices and to give you space to be challenged and respond

- In the appendices, we provide sample medium- and short-term lesson planning/evaluation pro formas, a language audit and sample lesson plans/evaluations.

In other words, the book can be read in a number of different ways, last of which is from front cover to back cover! That will work, of course, but our intention is to provide you with a resource that is flexible enough to cope with your individual needs.

But first a word about planning. Here is not the place to discuss in detail issues to do with planning – we assume that whatever kind of course you are doing will deal with that in generic terms or within the subject domain.

However, we do make some assumptions about planning that need to be specified. We hope you will find them useful in your discussions about planning with school/college mentors and university tutors.

Throughout the book, you will come across examples of lesson plans, many of which are based on real lesson plans created by trainee teachers as part of their training. So that you can see the main features of our view of planning, we also provide you with a blank template. Please feel free to adapt and amend it. No one yet has produced the perfect, all-purpose lesson plan that suits everyone. And thank goodness for that. Planning is something that has important idiosyncratic aspects to it, because we usually do it for ourselves and the plans will, to a greater or lesser extent, express something of our professional individuality. However, there are some essential features, namely:

- clear learning objectives ('By the end of this lesson, pupils will know/understand/be able to ... ')
- clear teaching objectives and strategies
- a sequence of lesson activities, including what teacher will do and what pupils will do
- use of variety – in pace, activity, learning styles, teaching styles, resources
- a rationale for the sequence that connects with understandings of the ways pupils learn
- consideration of resources, materials and technology
- planned assessment and monitoring opportunities
- a chance for pupils to reflect on their learning ('What have you learnt today? How do I know that?')
- a record of homework set
- 'memo to self' opportunities ('Remember to see Jayne's exercise book next lesson.' 'Start next lesson from No. 5 in this lesson plan – ran out of time for 6 and 7.' 'Make sure Kylie and Jason do not sit together in future!')
- a more considered and reflective lesson evaluation. (How effective was the learning and the teaching? What implications for the next lesson are there from this lesson? What changes to the next lesson plan will you make as a result of assessment and monitoring feedback in this lesson?)

We hope you find those comments helpful, and that they contribute to the development of your style of planning, for you and your pupils.

So, please feel free to dip in as appropriate, or be directed to a particular chapter by a mentor, or seek out lesson planning exemplars across a number of chapters, or tangle with the intellectual rationale for a view of literature, or whatever! We hope it caters for your needs.

THE USE OF 'TEXT'

We would be the first to admit that whenever there are two or three English/Literacy teachers together, there are always going to be some differences of opinion or emphasis about something! And we would be lying if we said to you that all the writers of this book agree about everything to do with English/Literacy.

But out of our debates, we have united around the notion of 'text', and, as it is such a fundamental concept in this book, it is worth spending a little time and space to introduce the idea at this early stage, so that references to 'texts' will be understood more clearly in later chapters.

We use the term 'text', first, to mean any occasion when language is used. That seems simple enough! And in essence it is. From the mundane to the earth-shattering, from the private to the public, from the conversational to the academic, from the polemic to the factual – all are texts. And they can exist in a variety of forms – from the permanent to the ephemeral, from the printed to the videoed, from the visual to the auditory.

Texts can also be visual, or largely dependent on sounds for their communication, or any mix from any or all of the available modes. So, the second essential prerequisite for a text is that it communicates – from pre-speech baby babblings to serious journalism, from the bathroom mirror monologue to the lecture hall presentation, from MTV to government information film, from website to billboard.

The scope for investigation and adaptation of texts is enormous, and forms part of the excitement of the subject. As we explore the texts of the past, so at the same time we accommodate the new texts of the present and future; the vogue for 'texting' via mobile telephones is a phenomenon as worthy of our attention as the impact of the printing press on literacy developments – both developments have had profound effects on our ability to create texts for means of communication. And, in passing, note that a new verb has entered the language: to text. The technological innovation has added to the language.

Later in the book there are fuller considerations of this matter, including the issue of quality, and whether it helps to see some texts as more 'valuable' than others. But for the moment, we hope you can grasp the concept with enthusiasm, and we trust that by the end of the course you are on, or by the time you get to the end of this book, or ideally both, that you see the possibilities for your teaching and pupils' learning in such a notion.

ESSENTIAL COMPANION DOCUMENTS

Throughout this volume, mention is made of a number of key documents. We recommend that you have easy access to the following:

- *The National Literacy Strategy* (DfEE, 1998) – the teaching and learning objectives for Reception to Year 6, which usefully contains the rationale for the view of literacy that informs the Strategy and the Framework
- *English: The National Curriculum for English* (DfEE, 1999) – the legal requirements for the teaching of English
- *Key Stage 3 National Strategy: Literacy across the Curriculum* (DfEE, 2001a) – the cross-curricular focus, with implications for English/Literacy teaching
- *Key Stage 3 National Strategy: Framework for Teaching English, Years 7, 8 and 9* (DfEE, 2001b) – the development of the National Literacy Strategy into secondary education.

The trouble with books is that they are not flexible enough to cope with changes as they happen – those amendments can only be made when a new edition is printed. So things will move on ahead of changes to this book, and you would do well to keep as up to date as possible with developments in the world of English/Literacy teaching and learning. Nevertheless, we offer the above titles as currently essential companion pieces to this volume.

One way to keep up to speed with changes is to access some websites. Again, the world of the Web is in constant flux, but currently we recommend:

- the Standards website, part of the Department for Education and Skills: http://www.standards.dfes.gov.uk
- the National Literacy Trust: http://www.literacytrust.org.uk

GLOSSARY

Education is a field of human endeavour that manages to generate as many acronyms and jargon/technical terms as any other, if not more. To that end, we have provided you with a glossary of terms following the end of this preface.

AND FINALLY ...

It would not be a proper preface if we did not acknowledge the help and support we have had in the writing of this book.

We have based the book on our collective experience of working with trainee teachers over many years in a great variety of contexts, and we wish to thank them for contributing in their many ways to the honing of our own practice as teacher educators.

We wish to thank our colleagues at Crewe and Didsbury who have been supportive of, and interested in, this venture. Many of them have contributed unwittingly to the book, by comments and thoughts, references to other books and materials, copies of templates – in lots of different ways.

Finally, we want to thank each other. What we mean is that this has been an enriching experience for all of us, in that we have had to articulate to each other our deeply held beliefs and philosophies about a subject we all hold very dear, both professionally and intellectually. We have also benefited from the exchanges, in that we have a stronger sense of what we agree on, and we all also recognize that there have been developments in our collective as well as individual thinking as a result of the process.

GLOSSARY OF TERMS

Below is an explanation of terms frequently used in the book, including any shorthand versions and acronyms used.

Term as used in the book	Explanation
Advanced level qualifications (A levels): AS and A2	Post-16 modular qualifications: Advanced Subsidiary (AS) taken in year one, Advanced level (AS+A2) after two years
Attainment Targets (ATs)	Designated areas of study in the National Curriculum – England. For English, these are Speaking and Listening (En1), Reading (En2) and Writing (En3)
Pupils learning English as an Additional Language (EAL learners)	Any pupil whose first language is not English. This will include early stage learners and advanced learners, UK and non-UK citizens
Framework for Teaching English: Years 7, 8 and 9 (the Framework)	The English component of the Key Stage 3 National Strategy, based closely on the revised National Curriculum for 2000, and designed to complement the current English Order
GCSE	General Certificate of Secondary Education: a set of subject-based assessments designed for the 14–16 age group in England, Wales, and Northern Ireland
Key Stages 1 to 4 (KS3, KS4)	The National Curriculum is organized into age-related phases covering ages 5–16 as follows: Kesy Stage 1 ages 5–7, Key Stage 2 ages 7–11, Key Stage 3 ages 11–14 and Key Stage 4 ages 14–16

Key Stage 3 National Strategy (the Strategy/ the KS3Strategy)	A government-led initiative to raise standards by strengthening teaching and learning across all subjects at Key Stage 3. For details of many training materials available in schools visit www.standards.dfes.gov.uk/keystage3
The National Association for the Teaching of English (NATE)	NATE is the UK subject teacher association for all aspects of English from pre-school to university. The association aims to support effective teaching and learning, to keep teachers informed about current developments and to provide them with a national voice (quoted from Summer 2002 edition of *English in Education*, the NATE journal)
National Curriculum: English (NC English, NC for English, English in the NC)	The current statutory English curriculum in schools in England. For details visit www.nc.uk.net
The National Literacy Strategy: framework for teaching (NLS)	A 5–11 primary literacy curriculum designed to raise standards through an objectives-led framework. Implemented in 1997, it influenced planning for the KS3 Framework
Qualifications and Curriculum Authority (QCA)	Government body that regulates developments in curriculum and assessment in schools, colleges and the workplace
Standard Assessment Tasks (SATs)	End of Key Stage assessments of achievement in English, Mathematics, and Science, taken in England and Wales (KS1 tasks not applicable in Wales)

CHAPTER ONE

Introduction: English and Literacy

In this chapter we attempt to define what we mean by the subject 'English'. Oddly enough, we have set ourselves a difficult task; if you think that what constitutes 'English' is obvious, straightforward, uncontested or incontestable, then be prepared for a shock.

What we aim to do is to provide you with an intellectually consistent, academically rigorous and professionally focused view of the subject. We believe that those three crucial aspects – the intellectual, the academic and the professional – are all interconnected, because it is out of the interplay of those elements that *what* we teach and *how* we teach English in secondary schools emerges.

ENGLISH: THE STORY CONTINUES

Now is not the time for another history of English as a subject worthy of study – others have done it very well already; for example, please see Davies (1996) and Marshall (2000). However, the nature of the subject in the years leading up to and following the arrival of the National Curriculum, and the attendant debates and disagreements, requires some account of history, if only to contextualize where we are now and what might happen to our understanding of the subject in the immediate future.

To get some idea of the current state of the subject, one only has to look at the names of the courses on offer in universities in the UK under the overarching title of English. There are courses called 'English Literature' and 'English Language' which for most of us are instantly recognizable as belonging to English.

At the other end of the scale of instant recognition, however, are courses with titles such as 'Contemporary Cultural Studies', 'Literatures in English', 'Media Studies' and many others that combine seemingly disparate elements of English into one course.

So, there is a rich variety of emphases in the academic world, and debates about 'What is English?' regularly burst into life. The analogy one might use is of an active volcano, mostly dormant, but occasionally terrorizing the locality with surprise eruptions of unpredictable duration.

There are some aspects of recent debates that need to be highlighted, for two main reasons:

- They have not gone away and you need to be ready for the next 'eruption'.
- They have been profoundly influential in defining the current conceptualization of the subject in secondary schools.

In 1989, Professor Brian Cox and his committee wrote the first version of English in the National Curriculum, *English for Ages 5 to 16*. In it, they recognized that English is perceived differently by teachers, and they defined five dominant emphases:

- personal growth
- cross-curricular
- adult needs
- cultural heritage
- cultural analysis (DES, 1989: paras 2.20–2.27).

We still find those definitions useful in a variety of ways:

- They can be helpful when looking at an English Department, to see if any views dominate.
- We can use them to chart our own intellectual development in the subject.
- We can use them to contextualize debates about the nature of the subject.

We can configure those views in a variety of ways. For example:

- Some views look inward to the individual (personal growth), while others look outward to the world of work (adult needs).

- Some see English as an educational requirement (cross-curricular), while others see it as part of a wider heritage (cultural heritage).

- Some views are concerned with enabling pupils to access significant aspects of their cultural history (cultural heritage), while others connect pupils with contemporary cultural manifestations in all their variety (cultural analysis).

- Some are about an initiation into an established set of texts (cultural heritage), while others are about understanding and critiquing the contemporary, the immediate, the influential, the ephemeral (cultural analysis).

(For further views on the above issues, please read Goodwyn, 1999.)

At the moment, English – as defined by National Curriculum requirements, examination syllabuses at GCSE and post-16, and recent initiatives in Literacy Education – requires learners to engage with all aspects of the five models of English:

- Personal growth – we can see that English involves not only the intellect, but also feelings. In addition, because of the nature of the texts in English, we have to deal with 'issues' in ways that develop our learners as people as well as students of English.

- Cross-curricular – cross-curricular literacy is back on the agenda, as teachers become more aware of the distinctive literacy demands of their subject, as well as seeing how the teaching and learning of literacy are inextricably intertwined with teaching and learning in their subject.

- Adult needs – we would all subscribe to the view that our learners need to be able to cope with the literacy demands of the workplace, as well as the wider issues of becoming informed and involved citizens who can communicate and be aware of how communications affect and influence. Such views are implemented in the curriculum through the focus on Key Skills at GCSE and A level.

- Cultural heritage – Shakespeare is still an author who has to be studied in secondary schools; indeed, that requirement has statutory status in Key Stages 3 and 4. In addition, GCSE and A level syllabuses draw in part on understandings of the literary heritage for their choices of examination texts.

■ Cultural analysis – the study of an aspect of the Media is a compulsory element in the GCSE examination, and A level syllabuses require learners to engage with recent and current literary critical theories.

WHERE ARE WE NOW?

Despite the views expressed above, it would be wrong to give the impression that peace and harmony have broken out. There are still echoes of previous reverberations, historical reminders of debates still unresolved. And you need to be aware of them, in order to understand the present as well as preparing you for what is to come.

We believe there are *four* major areas of continuing debate and disagreement:

1. Cultural heritage v. cultural analysis.

2. Standard English v. varieties of English (or 'Englishes').

3. Standards generally (the 'complaints tradition').

4. English *or* Literacy versus English *and* Literacy.

CULTURAL HERITAGE V. CULTURAL ANALYSIS

This debate is not going to go away, so we need to tackle it forcefully. We believe that it is not a case of either/or, but rather both. Yes, it is difficult to define the literary heritage – the so-called 'literary canon' – and, yes, it does keep changing and, yes, it is dominated by dead white males.

But there are some texts from the past, acknowledged as possessing some qualities, that our learners ought to experience. At the same time as we make 'great literature' accessible to our learners, we can also deconstruct the notion of the canon and examine its assumptions; for example, the texts exist to enable us to explore not only the male First World War poets, but also the writings of women at war and on the home front, and to ask the question: why have the male poets achieved canonical status, while the women's writing has not (yet)?

In terms of cultural analysis, there is so much richness in the range and variety of texts our learners experience constantly that it would be intellectually dishonest not to acknowledge the impact of advertising, tabloid newspapers, MTV, soap operas, pop music, the fashion industry – to name but a few – on the lives of our learners.

It is not a question of whether Shakespeare is better than *EastEnders*; let us study both, see the differences and similarities, and understand the contemporary appeal of both. Then we can consider how Shakespeare might have dealt with some of the issues raised in *EastEnders*, and then devise a soap opera version of *Romeo and Juliet*.

STANDARD ENGLISH V. VARIETIES OF ENGLISH

In strictly linguistic terms, standard English is a variety of English that has acquired a particular social and cultural status, as it is the English spoken and written in formal and educated contexts. However, there are some who believe that standard English is the best kind of English, thus implying that other kinds of English are inferior and less desirable.

Such a view is intellectually untenable. In addition, acting upon that view can have deleterious effects on our learners, especially those who bring other varieties of English to our classrooms. We need to remember that such pupils, for many of whom standard English is an unknown quantity, bring the English of their geographical area or country of origin, or the English of their social class or cultural heritage, or the dominant forms of English in their families, to our classrooms. We need to understand the connections between language and identity, however defined. We need to deal sensitively with non-standard and dialect forms as we take on the responsibility and curriculum requirement to teach our learners to use Standard English as appropriate.

Ideally, we want our learners to have a range of Englishes that they can draw on as appropriate; we want our learners to code-switch, appreciate the richness of the registers of contemporary English and to appreciate how language defines them as individuals with culture, history and uniqueness.

In addition, we want our learners to understand that all varieties of English can be described, and that we can investigate the rules that govern usage, while at the same time adding to many learners' repertoires the benefits of being able to use standard English.

STANDARDS GENERALLY (THE 'COMPLAINTS TRADITION')

Let us start with an incontrovertible statement: since the dawning of English as a language in its own right, standards of usage have never been good enough for somebody. The so-called 'complaints tradition' continues to have its baleful influence on debates about standards. We guarantee that within a few weeks of searching in newspapers, listening to or watching the news, or conversations 'around the water cooler', you will come across someone complaining about the language children use these days, or standards of spelling, or use of slang, or people's accents, or handwriting, or the fact that children 'don't read books anymore', or whatever.

Such moments are worth collecting for use with your learners, as they ably illustrate a linguistic phenomenon, namely, that language is in a constant state of flux, that usage changes over time and that many people do not like change. Indeed, they assume – wrongly – that language is a constant, that it ought to be unchanging, and that change equals falling standards and the beginnings of the end of civilization.

The truth is quite different; historically, language has always been changing, in our case heavily influenced by other languages brought here by invaders. In addition, traders and colonizers have brought back to English words and phrases from the languages of the regions they have visited.

As well as those influences, we have to acknowledge that usage changes over time. For example, there are many people who still make a distinction between 'less work' and 'fewer jobs', 'less' taking a singular noun, whereas 'fewer' needs a plural noun. However, we regularly hear and read 'less' used in both circumstances, as 'There are less jobs in the steel industry these days.'

We can complain all we like, shout at the television and write letters to *The Times*, but in the end usage will win. The change is not linguistically qualitative – the loss of the distinction will not damage the language or make certain things 'unsayable', but it is a change nevertheless.

Such changes are all around us, and our learners know a lot about, for example, the latest slang 'in' words for 'good' or 'bad', as in historical examples such as 'fab', 'ace', 'brill', 'wicked' and so on. We can devise ways of exploring loan words from particular languages and cultures, and learners for whom English is a second or third language can initiate us into the practices and conventions of their distinctive ways of reading and writing.

Once again, we conclude in this instance that change is a reason for exploration and celebration, contributing to an intellectual and academic tradition that describes rather than prescribes, and that analyses within a rule-governed framework rather than using archaic rules to circumscribe language use.

ENGLISH OR/AND LITERACY

Literacy is a fairly new arrival on the secondary English stage. Until very recently, the term 'literacy' would normally be applied to early years' teaching, to adult classes in basic literacy or to national and international tests of reading and writing. You will also see the plural form used in recent books about the teaching of English – as in electronic or media literacies. This usage acknowledges the complexity and multiplicity of literacy practices in a global context (see Chapter 2 for a discussion of critical literacy).

For at least thirty years English teachers have thought their 'territory' was defined as reading, writing, speaking and listening. So how is it that literacy has become such a strong presence that it appears in the title of this book? The answer lies with government educational initiatives in England and Wales (but most particularly in England) since 2001.

The introduction of the Key Stage 3 National Strategy in 2001 involved a major school-wide push to prioritize literacy teaching in all subjects. The Strategy was explicitly designed to sustain and extend curriculum programmes begun in the primary phase, notably the National Literacy Strategy (DfEE, 1998). The Key Stage 3 Strategy was supported by an ambitious and practical curriculum guidance pack called *Literacy across the Curriculum* (DfEE, 2001a), to be explored further in Chapter 2. For English teachers, the core National Strategy document is *Framework for Teaching English: Years 7, 8 and 9* (DfEE, 2001b). Look at how literacy makes its first appearance in the Framework – a key working document for your training year.

These are the opening words of the Rationale and Introduction:

> The Key Stage 3 National Strategy is part of the government's commitment to raise standards in schools. Effective literacy is the key to raising standards across all subjects, and equipping pupils with the skills and knowledge they need for life beyond school.
>
> **(DfEE, 2001b: 9)**

You should note the word associations here: *government* wants to raise *standards*, and raising standards equals improving *literacy*. These associations explain why the English curriculum is central to national educational debates – and why English teachers play for such high stakes!

And what does the government mean by 'effective literacy'? The Rationale and Introduction goes on to hitch literacy to the more familiar English curriculum by equating 'sophisticated literacy skills' with 'a shrewd and fluent independent reader, a confident writer and an effective speaker and listener' (DfEE, 1999: 10). Literacy teaching, then, is good holistic English teaching across the four modes of reading, writing, speaking and listening.

That said, literacy has become a significant political discourse during the past few years and English teachers and their professional associations have had to become familiar with its vocabulary (see, for example, Haworth, 2002). There are those who fear that literacy teaching points to a dull, objectives-led curriculum with teachers worried about curriculum coverage rather than exciting content (see Allen, 2002; Wrigley 2003; and the discussion in Chapter 10). Others have suggested literacy teaching excludes those with differing language backgrounds (King, 2002).

We believe that we have engaged with some of these tensions in the following chapters, but with an international readership in mind – and a wish to remain true to the principled evolution of the English secondary curriculum – we have chosen to align our discussions in this book with the established four interlinked modes of reading, writing, speaking and listening.

Finally, all the research surveys we have encountered reach the conclusion that there is no evidence that standards of learners' achievements in English are falling; for example, the most recent international comparison, produced by the Organization for Economic Co-operation and Development (OECD), rates England in the top rank of countries, prompting the then Secretary of State for Education, Estelle Morris, to comment in a press release on 4 December 2001 that:

> The Programme for International Student Assessment (PISA), run by the Organisation for Economic Co-operation and Development (OECD), surveyed 265,000 students in 32 countries during 2000. It assessed the ability of 15 year olds to apply their knowledge and skills in reading, mathematical and scientific literacy to real life problems, rather than measuring the extent to which students have mastered particular school subjects.
>
> The study – the most comprehensive international survey ever undertaken – shows that England's results across all three areas of reading, mathematical and scientific literacy were significantly above the OECD average … .
>
> **(For the full text of the press release, please go to:**
> http://www.dfes.gov.uk/pns/DisplayPN.cgi?pn_id=2001_0404)

That is no excuse for complacency, but at least the research evidence presents us with the pedagogic challenge of how improvements can be maintained.

A TEXTUAL VIEW OF ENGLISH

If you think that the above is some sort of woolly, liberal thinking, we want now to ground our views in a particular conceptualization of the subject English which has direct relevance for pedagogic practice in secondary schools.

You may have noticed that the word 'text' is used above quite a lot. The word needs defining more closely, as for many of us the word 'text' means that particular kind of literary work chosen by examination boards for study. We want to expand the notion of text so that it incorporates the variety of ways we can communicate using English.

There are written texts and spoken texts. Written texts have a degree of permanence associated with print. But we also want to develop the idea of a written text into the area of something deliberately created to communicate with others via some kind of physical record, document or presence. If we do that, then visual texts and 'moving image texts' (a phrase taken from the current version of the National Curriculum document) become texts within the same definition. Therefore, anything that uses language and is the outcome of choices and decisions becomes a text. Great writers make choices, and so do film editors, advertising copywriters and drama directors – and so do we, every time we choose our words carefully, so as not to offend a family member, or to speak appropriately to the headteacher, or reply to a question at an interview for a position we really want very badly. Making choices goes to the heart of creating texts, of whatever kind.

Spoken texts are usually understood to be primarily ephemeral. We can regard the conversation about last night's television programme in the common room, for example, as a spoken text, in the sense that there was communication, using language, and where the participants made choices about words to use, tone of voice, volume and so on.

But it is essentially ephemeral, in that it does not last much beyond the moment. It would be difficult to do much with it unless the conversation were recorded and possibly transcribed onto paper or a computer screen. By recording and transcribing we can give a spoken text some permanence, thus making it easier to preserve it and to explore its linguistic features.

In recent years another type of text has made its entry – the digital text. Digital texts share some features with permanent texts while at the same time being more malleable than print on paper. When a digital text is loaded into a word processor, blocks of text can be moved around, designated words replaced with others, and the general look of the text (for example, choice of font style and size, layout on the page) can be altered.

Some digital texts have very distinctive features. A web page with click points, for example, has a different organization from a book. Digital texts need not be accessed sequentially, page after page; they allow for a more idiosyncratic usage that may lack the usual page-turning sequence. Other examples of digital texts could include:

■ digital presentations, using software such as Microsoft's

PowerPoint

- electronic newspapers
- emails
- mobile phone text messages
- Internet chat rooms.

All the types of text defined above – written, spoken, digital – share some common features:

- They all use language in a great variety of ways.
- They are all the products of choices about language, format and genre.
- They all intend to communicate.
- They all conform to a set of descriptive rules that define the type of text.

It is our view that if we put the notion of 'text' at the centre of English, then everything else falls into place. The National Curriculum, as well as dividing English into the Attainment Targets (ATs) of Speaking and Listening, Reading, and Writing, also sees English as made up of distinctive elements:

- language
- literature
- drama
- media
- information and communication technology (ICT).

To avoid too much fragmentation, and to implement the pleas in the National Curriculum for a holistic view of the subject, we need some mechanism for marrying the Attainment Targets (ATs), the elements of English and the notion of text.

We think the argument goes like this:

- The ATs define the learning that has to take place.
- The elements of English provide a rich variety of very different and distinctive resources for those learning objectives.
- Those resources are essentially a range of texts, providing models, opportunities to explore and replicate.

So, when we talk about, for example, Language, we talk about a range of language texts. Many of us are familiar with the fact that Literature is made up of different genres of texts, with sub-genres for each genre however defined. Drama texts – whether written/published or the outcomes of performed improvisations – have a set of distinctive features that justifies the inclusion of Drama on those terms alone. We have already mentioned the idea of Media texts as having a distinctive set of features, and they share with ICT or digital texts the regular combination of sounds and pictures, still or moving, with words, spoken or written.

The pedagogic implication of the above goes like this: we choose the texts to set before our learners with learning objectives in mind. Those objectives are defined by the *National Curriculum for English* (DfEE, 1999) and currently the *Framework for Teaching English: Years 7, 8 and 9* (DfEE, 2001b). The sequence of thinking is therefore:

- What will the learners learn?
- What textual resources shall I use/provide to effect that learning?
- What outcomes from the lessons and associated activities will provide me, the teacher, with evidence of the learners' learning?

There is no hierarchy in the list of elements of English – all five are there because they provide different kinds of texts, and we owe it to our learners to take advantage for their sakes of that variety. Some of the debates about English still survive in this conceptualization, and it is not our intention to suggest that our view neutralizes those discussions once and for all. Indeed, we all feel that it is constantly exciting to be working in a subject area where the debates and discussions are so lively, heartfelt and endless.

Nevertheless, we also argue that what we are proposing here is consistent with current understandings of best pedagogic practice in the teaching of English/Literacy. None of us wants to take the heart and soul out of the subject, nor are we advocating a reductive skills-based approach to teaching and learning in English. Rather, we are convinced that the view of the subject presented here can lead to quality teaching and learning, so that pupils can gain control of the language, can make appropriate linguistic and textual choices, and can decide what they want to communicate and how best to communicate it.

CHAPTER TWO

Language Study

INTRODUCTION

> The importance of English today, however, is increasingly that of a world language, spoken by people who have a wide range of different histories and cultural allegiances. Many of these will have first encountered English as a world language not through its literary heritage, but through the global dissemination of American popular culture.
>
> (Maybin, 2000: 192)

Most candidates applying for places on English Postgraduate Certificate of Education (PGCE) secondary courses write about their love of literature and their wish to communicate this passion to future generations. Very few speak of their love of the English language in quite the same way. This chapter will ask you to examine both your personal relationship with language and your professional knowledge and understanding of its role in English teaching. You are asked to consider whether English teaching should be constituted of literature and language teaching in roughly equal measure (with media, drama and ICT supporting each of these 'elements of English') and to investigate how the balance is maintained in your placement schools. We will also develop the idea of 'text' as presented in Chapter 1.

LANGUAGE AND IDENTITY

First we will consider our personal investment in the English language, whether as a 'first' language or 'second' language speaker. In an increasingly plurilingual world, this rich diversity in both teacher and learner repertoire becomes part of the canvas upon which we draw when teaching.

To realize how acutely our identities are tied into language, we need only think of how we feel when our chosen names or titles are misused or mispronounced. Some might recall the acute feelings associated with having an accent, dialect or language different from the majority in a particular social setting – be it in the school playground or the workplace. Consider, too, how modes of address convey subtle distinctions in interpersonal relations and how offensive language is carefully graded by its users to maximize hurt.

What interpersonal relations are defined by the word choices highlighted in the following?

Woman/girl/lady/madam
Lad/boy/sir/mister/man/gentleman

And why is woman less readily used than man to describe the gender group?

These instances point to the crucial link between language and power. The language we use helps to shape social practice, carrying the inflections of power in so many of our daily encounters – those between employer and employee, teacher and pupil, parent and child, for example. During school experience, note whether the headteacher is referred to as 'the head', 'the boss' or even 'the management' in the staffroom. If the nameplate on the head's door says 'headmaster/mistress', might you expect a heavily gendered school culture – or at least a culture where social issues go unchallenged? And what social/pedagogic messages are conveyed if a teacher refers to boys collectively as 'lads'? Or a teacher asks for 'Christian' names for the register? As others have said, 'We are what we communicate'. As teachers, we have a particular responsibility to use language thoughtfully and inclusively – and that includes the written texts we bring into the classroom.

The implications of the language–power axis for teaching professionals are fully theorized in what has become known as critical discourse analysis, associated with the work of Norman Fairclough amongst others (see, for example, Fairclough, 1992; 2001). In these writings you will find accessible examples illustrating how dominant social groups use language to determine and control, at least partly, the events and people in their sphere of influence. If language carries such potency, then it is surely the business of the English teacher to ensure that pupils' language repertoires are developed and sustained so that they leave school with the knowledge and the experience to function confidently as language users.

LANGUAGE AND THE SECONDARY TEACHER

In an ambitious attempt to define language education in the broadest possible terms for British educators in the twenty-first century, Brumfit (1995) proposed four entitlements for all learners:

- To develop their mother tongue or dialect to maximum confident and effective use.

- To develop competence in a range of styles of English for educational, work-based social and public-life purposes.

- To develop their knowledge of how language operates in a multilingual society, including basic experiences of languages other than their own that are significant either in education or in the local community.

- To develop as extensive as possible a practical competence in at least one language other than their own.

Do you agree that this 'language charter' for schools is appropriate for schools in the UK today? How much does the NC for English address? Which aspects do you think are most challenging to schools and which do you think might be neglected?

Have recent government policies supported or weakened this entitlement?

Might the response to these proposals be different according to your personal language history? Might governmental priorities vary across nations?

At the beginning of the twenty-first century, all secondary teachers are being asked to support their school's identified literacy targets generated by an ambitious Key Stage 3 National Strategy to locate literacy, numeracy and ICT as cross-curricular priorities for all teachers (DFEE, 2001a). The *Literacy across the Curriculum* (LAC) folder contains rigorous and creative materials for departmental training on such topics as the management of group talk, making notes, writing non-fiction and spelling and vocabulary. Taken as a whole, this folder provides a challenging agenda for departments to develop their pedagogic knowledge of how language can be made to support effective learning in all subjects.

> Having looked at the LAC folder more closely, you might want to consider whether 'language' could have replaced 'literacy' in the title. What areas of specialist language knowledge is the folder drawing upon? Look, for example, at the chapter 'Reading for Information'. Do you think English teachers would normally have such knowledge about reading strategies? Are these realistic expectations of all secondary teachers?

English teachers may well be expected to underpin whole school initiatives in this area and the available materials would certainly sustain a rich professional dialogue for several years. (At the time of writing, complementary materials for secondary foundation subjects are being published – DfES, 2002a.) Much of the content is as useful for English departments in strengthening and consolidating best practice as it is likely to be innovative for other departments. Unless secondary teachers are given time to explore their own understandings of how language works in, say, the composition of a science report or a humanities essay, they will not have the confidence to communicate this knowledge to pupils in effective ways. Of particular importance is the relationship between spoken language and literacy in sustaining learning. It is pleasing to see separate chapters devoted to the management of group talk and listening skills, explicitly linked to effective learning, but teachers need considerable departmental time to consolidate their own appreciation of these subtle processes, if they are to have any lasting impact on classroom practice.

> During school placements, investigate how senior management teams are developing 'literacy' as a whole school initiative. Then explore the role of the English department in this initiative. Try to distinguish between the department's cross-curricular responsibility and their English-specific agenda for literacy.
>
> Then compare the school's wider language curriculum with the 'charter' referred to earlier.

LANGUAGE AND THE ENGLISH TEACHER

▥ SOME KEY CONSIDERATIONS

What does an English teacher need to know about language? As an experienced user of English you already have vast reserves of *implicit knowledge* about language. Any native speaker is an instinctive grammarian in her/his own language, having immediate access to appropriate word order, verb formations, word agreements and irregular wording. The native speaker would not say 'mouses', 'I runned', 'I go to home', but these are all 'logical' possibilities if you are learning English as an additional language. If you have tried learning another language, you will appreciate how easy it is to make similar mistakes when translating from your home language. What we need to consider here is the extent and purpose of *explicit knowledge* about language which English teachers need to have. And, following from this, what explicit knowledge should we expect our pupils to acquire?

Consider also two mutually supportive approaches to language study in the classroom:

- investigation of language as a social and cultural phenomenon
- close linguistic analysis of any given text.

The first might invite you to explore how language changes over time and how many dialect words are still used in a local area; the second approach might study how dialect and non-standard forms are used in a particular poem to create effects. It is likely that any trainee teacher feeling a certain shudder at the mention of language knowledge will have thought only of the analytic dimension of language study – often called 'grammar teaching'. Anyone educated after the 1960s will probably have had little experience of formal grammar teaching – even those of us with such a background are likely to have mixed feelings about its value. (The following chapter is devoted to a discussion of grammar teaching.)

Holding on to these broad distinctions, we will now trace, in outline, how the secondary English language curriculum has developed over the past thirty years in order to help you locate your personal experience, if educated in the English 'system' – and to alert you to its highly contested position in the English classroom (Figure 2.1).

1950s–1970s	Language teaching was mostly interpreted as clause analysis, teaching parts of speech etc.
1971	Doughty, Thornton et al. produced *Language in Use* – a language resource for teachers based on Hallidayan grammar which put 'language in use' before 'language analysis', e.g. units on 'language in society'
1975	*The Bullock Report – A Language for Life*. Significant forerunner of Kingman and Cox reports. It took a holistic view of language, emphasizing language as an issue for all teachers and its role in learning
1984	English from 5–16: Inspectorate's first attempt to define a national curriculum for English in *Curriculum Matters* (parallel papers for each subject), appearing to hint at a return to old style grammar teaching
1986	Responses to *Curriculum Matters* – outcry from English teachers acknowledged – suggestion that an inquiry be set up to draw up recommendations about what might be taught about language to intending teachers
1988	Kingman committee established in response. It produced a detailed descriptive model of language, not 'old style' prescriptive grammar. Made recommendations for attainment targets for Knowledge about Language (KAL) at 7, 11 and 16
1989	The Cox Report – took up Kingman's framework *Knowledge about Language* (KAL) and tried to offer pedagogic interpretation
1989–92	Language in the National Curriculum (LINC) project – government-funded project to produce materials to support the implementation of KAL teaching as proposed in Kingman and Cox – government refused permission to publish LINC training materials
1992–95	Draft revisions of National Curriculum English ('battles' over definitions and role of Standard English and grammar teaching)
1998–99	Qualifications and Curriculum Authority (QCA) publish several papers designed 'to provide guidance on teaching the NC grammar requirements' and to 'promote and inform wider professional discussion of grammar teaching': '*The Grammar Papers*', '*Not Whether but How* ', '*Improving Writing at Key Stages 3 and 4*'
2000	NC English has greater integration of standard English within Attainment Targets, referring specifically to Language Structure and Language Variation
2001	*The Framework for Teaching English: Years 7, 8 and 9* Specific objectives relating to the teaching of grammar: word-, sentence- and text-level grammar

2.1 MILESTONES ON THE LANGUAGE ROAD

Can you detect the tensions between competing ways of looking at language? Which 'milestones' do you recognize from your own education and from any subsequent classroom experience?

▓ LANGUAGE STUDY IN THE NATIONAL CURRICULUM

Note the several changes to the way this area of study has been labelled in National Curriculum documents since 1989. It began life as *Knowledge about Language* (KAL), was renamed *Standard English and Language Study* in the 1995 English Orders, before being repackaged in 1999 as *Language Structure and Language Variation*. You might guess that these renamings were more than cosmetic changes. The 'promotion' of standard English in the 1995 Orders reflected a very public and politicized battle for the territory of English. The connotations of language with power were once again evident as teachers were exhorted to 'correct' children's English in the playground and to promote standard and 'appropriate' English over the study of linguistic forms and global variation. (To read more about this history and to 'walk the road' presented in Figure 2.1, see Carter, 1990; 1997; Cox, 1995.)

We will complete the review of national position statements concerning the role of language in English with reference to the *Framework for Teaching English: Years 7, 8 and 9* (DfEE, 2001b). The Framework is designed to support the NC for English by providing a more explicit model for language teaching derived from *The National Literacy Strategy* (DfEE, 1998) for primary schools. NC Attainment Targets are incorporated into a comprehensive set of teaching objectives listed as word-, sentence- and text-level objectives, in that order. It has been argued that text-level objectives should precede and subsume word- and sentence-level objectives. To refer back to an earlier distinction, the foregrounding of word- and sentence-level language study implies a privileging of micro-linguistic analysis over holistic investigation. But there is no doubt that the greater challenge for most secondary English teachers lies with word and sentence analysis – a theme of the next chapter.

Now explore the NC for English to see how language study is mapped across the three NC Attainment Targets of Speaking and Listening, Reading and Writing. Note what is included under these headings:

Standard English, Language variation/language structure, Understanding the author's craft, Punctuation, Spelling.

Then look for these headings in the Framework and read objectives listed under each heading. You should find that the Framework objectives provide clear prompts to support language study in the classroom. This exercise should help you complete the language audit in Appendix 1.

Having completed this exercise, it is quite likely that you came across terminology that caused you an anxious moment (perhaps less so for graduates in languages/linguistics). Maybe you felt uncertain about morphology, etymology, auxiliary or passive verb forms. Your feelings will tell you something about the power of terminology to affect the self-esteem of a language-user. Whilst it is important that you learn about the structure of language during your training, it is also essential that you recognize your implicit understanding of, say, auxiliary or passive verb forms in countless daily verbal interactions. When a pupil says 'the book got damaged, miss', she/he is instinctively selecting the passive verb form to avoid admitting personal blame: when you reply 'did you say who damaged the book?' you instinctively select the auxiliary 'did' to bring other meanings into play. This kind of word play is both sophisticated and commonplace for all proficient language users, including the children you will teach – consider the role language plays in playground jokes. So, whilst you complete the Language Audit, view the exercise as an agenda for making explicit what is already known – and for adding to your curiosity, knowledge and love for the language you already use fluently. At all costs, we want you to avoid presenting language study to your pupils from a deficit model, as a corrective exercise or an exposure of ignorance. (We will consider this key point in more detail in the next chapter.)

AUDITING SUBJECT KNOWLEDGE ABOUT LANGUAGE

Now turn to the Language Audit in Appendix 1, organized as three themes:

1. Language as spoken and written system.
2. Language as social, cultural and historical phenomenon.
3. Language in texts/discourse.

What to do with the findings from this audit?

1. Prepare to become an interested 'scholar of language' throughout your career, by finding some 'answers' to the gaps you have identified. You will need to refer to the reading lists at the end of this chapter and the next. You will find 'answers' in several ways: you might want to find a working definition of a given term by referring to the glossary in *Improving Writing at Key Stage 3 and 4* (QCA, 1999b); or you might want to broaden your awareness of standard English usage by reading the relevant chapter in one of the recommended texts.
2. Keep this audit in mind when you visit schools. You must consolidate professional reading with practical experiences. Having read

---

about co-ordination and subordination in sentences, for example, you will need to see it being taught and to try it out for yourself. You might even find that 'working definitions' do not quite 'work' when faced with pupils' responses! Add any such practical experiences to your audit, as vital evidence of learning about language.

3. Continue to read from the suggested reading lists throughout your training, and beyond, to become this interested 'scholar of language'. Remember the appeal made at the start of this chapter that you consider whether English teaching ought to draw as much on language sources as on literature.

LANGUAGE STUDY IN ENGLISH CLASSROOMS: MAPPING THE TERRITORY

First, let us look at some examples of language investigations that we recommend for use in the classroom, before providing any further maps to help you explore the 'language territory'. These activities will comfortably fit within the first approach to language study noted earlier – the broad investigation of language as 'social and cultural phenomenon'. As in other chapters, we will turn to the National Curriculum Attainment Targets to provide the 'grid references'.

LANGUAGE STUDY IN SUPPORT OF SPEAKING AND LISTENING

(Most of the activities listed below will, of course, also embrace the other two Attainment Targets.)

• *Pupils in role: making excuses to teachers/persuading parents to support an unlikely project/avoiding the difficult questions at home/moving between social groups*

What language choices are evident in these dialogues? (Similar dialogues are used in A level Language for close linguistic analysis.)

• *A day in the life of ... a secondary student ... a tutor group*

(Speaking to a teacher, parent, younger sibling, doing a presentation in school, text messaging, phoning an employer, buying or selling, arguing, socializing, negotiating, etc.)

Class discussion about the range of language which a secondary school pupil or group might use/experience in a day. Groups decide how they might represent this as a radio programme/drama/or display.

• *A language walk – presentation of findings*

Pupils have to list all the print they might come across from the minute they wake to the time they reach the school gates – they are invited to categorize this list.

OR

Pupils select five 'interesting' texts from their 'home–school walk' to make a collage/montage poem – discuss how the texts work/why they were chosen.

• *Formal/informal language*

To make the connection with informal/formal dress, pupils are asked to list what they'd wear on a variety of occasions, e.g., wedding, interview, meeting girl/boyfriend's parents, night out, etc. They are then asked to talk/write about how they would talk in each circumstance. (Teacher might have to be specific about contexts.)

OR

Teacher illustrates how she/he might change his/her language register, e.g., talking to a friend about teaching and presenting an argument to a school management meeting. Pupils list the differences and then try a similar exercise.

OR

Newspaper pictures – pupils select five pictures of 'contrasting' people (not famous). They have to decide how these people will speak. Pairs are formed and pupils have to interact in role; this can lead to script/story writing.

▧ LANGUAGE STUDY IN SUPPORT OF READING

  • *Using 'quality' picture books to investigate language use – those that make best use of text and image. (Such picture books for young children provide a rich resource for secondary teachers/pupils.)*

Examples:

Burningham's *Don't go near the water, Shirley.* How does written text and visual text relate?

How does McKee create humour in *Not Now Bernard*?

Compare an oral version of a traditional story with a written version, both orthodox and unorthodox – *Snow White* with *Snow White in New York* by F. French or *The Three Little Pigs* with *The True Story of the Three Little Pigs by A Wolf* by J.Scieszka.

- *Special interest magazines/books: glossaries*

Class sample non-fiction texts to explore the language/specialist terms used to produce glossaries for 'the lay reader'. Each class member/group has to provide a specialist text, usually a magazine, e.g., football fanzine magazines/extreme sports/computer games/fashion/music.

- *Language change – readings from Beowulf to Sir Gawain to Chaucer to Shakespeare*

(Essential to listen to tapes here, so supportive of Speaking and Listening too). Pupils/groups compile vocabulary lists or diagrams to show changes over time.

▨ LANGUAGE STUDY IN SUPPORT OF WRITING

- *Parallel stories*

Pupils are asked to create a story which tells about two very different people who do not interact in the story but are linked in some way, e.g., an infant child's morning at school and her/his headteacher, e.g., a politician talking about unemployment and a 17-year-old on a training scheme. The story should show different registers of language.

- *Mixed genre stories*

Groups collaborate to write a story in chapters; each chapter must be written in a different genre, e.g., cartoon format/diary/playscript/ansaphone message/formal report/poem/letter/brochure/newspaper report.

The storyline must remain coherent throughout. *The Jolly Postman* (J. and A. Ahlberg) is an original and exquisite example to give inspiration.

- *Language autobiography*

The idea is that children try to tell the story of their lives from a language perspective rather than an historical perspective, e.g., trying to find out what people said and wrote when they were born – hospital name tags, birth announcements in newspapers, etc.

It can be depersonalized to investigate a whole group's language development, e.g., how did we learn to read/write – examples of the class's earliest writing; a class survey of books we loved when we were 7.

Any of these activities can stimulate pupils' curiosity about 'the world of language' and about the English language specifically, whilst meeting many NC objectives along the way. Taught appropriately, language study of this kind can enthuse able and less able, both boys and girls, infants and sixth-formers to appreciate the history and the richness of what they so easily take for granted – the very languages that sustain almost everything they do in the public domain. To secure this large claim about the role of language in English classrooms, teachers need to feel confident in relating actual practice to appropriate models of language to ensure coherence in planning and teaching.

SOME WAYS OF LOOKING AT LANGUAGE STUDY

Consider first an approach used by the Language in the National Curriculum (LINC) Project 1989–92 to explore the macro-functions of language. The LINC Project identified the following categories for language study:

- language variety
- language and society
- language acquisition and development
- history of language
- language as system.

It is also worth noting here that the A level English Language syllabuses use very similar categories to underpin their curriculum. The LINC Project was also instrumental in establishing the principles for language study in the National Curriculum and for disseminating good practice through local education authorities (LEAs) at a national level (see Carter, 1990).

Using these categories, locate some of the classroom activities listed in the previous section.

Now look at Figure 2.2, again adopted from the LINC Project (Carter, 1990) which provides a framework for understanding how a specific text might be studied within a broader linguistic framework, drawing on functional theories of language.

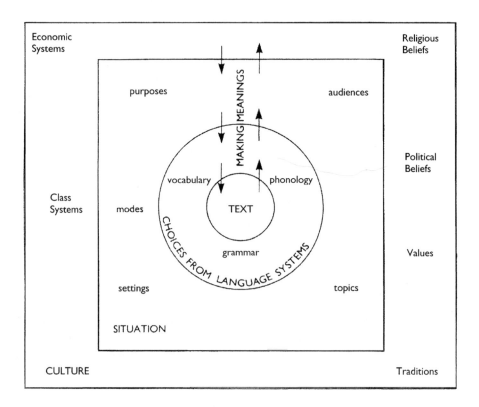

2.2 LOCATING TEXT WITHIN BROADER SOCIAL AND CULTURAL FRAMES
Source: Carter 1990: 9.

(For a fuller discussion of the theoretical underpinnings of the model in Figure 2.2, see Carter, 1990: Introduction.) The model attempts to explain how any text is linked to wider social and cultural patterns. It suggests we should not study words or texts in isolation, that meanings are not 'made' by the text but by the speaker or writer struggling to express her/his purpose to a particular audience (the middle box) within a specific cultural context with its values and expectations (the outer box). It should help you appreciate how difficult it can seem, for many pupils, to produce their own texts – if 'text' is so dependent on other larger choices and social experience.

If this sounds remote from classroom experience, let us consider an example. Consider Year 9 pupils doing a Key Stage 3 English test. They have to write a leaflet aimed at adolescents to persuade them to take seriously the need for conservation and environmental action to protect the planet. What resources will pupils draw on to produce this leaflet or 'text'? The second circle 'Choices from Language Systems' presents the technical choices we all make when preparing a text; the inexperienced speaker/writer will draw on the models taken from her/his teacher and from the 'texts' encountered in daily life. However, these choices are, in turn, influenced by our appreciation of social context – the 'situation' box in Figure 2.2. Our Year 9 pupils will only write effectively if they select the vocabulary, sentence structure and communication style they judge to be effective with an adolescent audience. If they are confident in making these selections, it is likely that their teacher has provided plenty of explicit experience in reading the genre of texts, their purposes and target audiences. And to achieve the highest marks, the conservation leaflet will have to be informed by a broader awareness of 'how the world is thinking about conservation' – the outer box in Figure 2.2. The leaflet might refer to the differing views of 'developed' and 'developing' countries or the 'green' protest movements that some young people join; it might make an emotional appeal about endangered species or ecosensitive lifestyles.

These sophisticated challenges apply as much to spoken texts as to the reading of texts produced by others. The conceptual framework presented in this section should provide you with both a principled rationale and the analytic tools for the two approaches to language study proposed earlier, that is, close textual analysis and broader social investigations of language use. Using these two approaches as reference points, we shall next map the territory still further, to highlight other significant features for the teacher of English.

> When you next have to prepare a 'significant text', try to use Figure 2.2 to illustrate the way you produce a text. It might be an oral presentation for a seminar or interview, a course assignment, a private letter, or a memo or email. Use the Year 9 test example above to guide you in locating your own experience within Figure 2.2.

LANGUAGE VARIATION

An obvious principle to draw from our discussion of Figure 2.2 is that of language variation. As producers of texts (writers and speakers) we will have many differing locations in that diagram which will shape our language choices, and as 'receivers' of others' texts (through reading and listening) we will also 'read' differently. For example, your gender, ethnicity, age and class will be highly significant in your formation and reception of texts – differently so for each individual – depending on which of the categories we invest in for identity. As you read the text below, reflect on how it communicates its cultural values and how it constructs its audience. Are you cast as an insider or outsider by the writer's language choices? Does the writer give you clues as to his own history, his cultural values – perhaps unintentionally? Do you read as revealing, the occasional literary narrative quirks and formal language choices? Your answers will depend on your investment in some of the significant categories noted above.

> We skated most of the evening. It was cold but I think our cores had been warmed by the sun from today and the promise of tomorrow. Nick killed a super-tight flat bank with an anchor protruding from its platform – switch ollie blunts and piv' fakies were raked back in over its rough surface. We skated a road island with trannie banks in the centre, then onto a super high rail which hid itself away in the darkness at the side of a theatre or something similar. Derek Beer crushed it with an absinthe-fuelled crook. It was on – it was all on!
>
> **(Extract from Document Skateboard, June 2002 – Percy Dean)**

The NC for English makes very specific references to the study of language variation through the Attainment Targets for Speaking and Listening and for Reading. The brief extract quoted above provides data for several of these proposed areas for study at secondary English:

En1 Speaking and Listening

- The importance of standard English.
- Current influences on spoken and written language.
- Attitudes to language use.
- Differences between speech and writing.
- Vocabulary and grammar of standard English and dialect variations.
- The development of English, including changes over time, borrowings from other languages, origins of words, and the impact of electronic communication on written language.

En2 Reading

- Pupils should be taught to draw on their knowledge of grammar and language variation to develop their understanding of texts and how language works.

Now consider the following sequences of lessons taught by trainee teachers to KS3 pupils. What aspects of National Curriculum language variation might these lessons explore?

1. A trainee uses audiotaped extracts from *Beowulf, Sir Gawain and the Green Knight* and *Canterbury Tales* as a listening exercise to lead to original writing based on these models.

2. A trainee investigates the etymology of words through various games activities: Call my Bluff, The Language House (groups visit language groups in their 'houses' to find out how English has borrowed words from other cultures – Dutch, Indian, Chinese, Scandinavian, etc.).

3. A trainee transcribes a bit of dialogue between her own toddler children and asks the class to look for the clues in the dialogue that distinguish the very young speaker.

If taught well, these lessons might touch on accent and dialect, historical change, the evolving standardization of English, language and power across the globe, spoken and written English, language acquisition and literary devices in Old English poetry. All these trainee teachers found pupils to be interested in these topics – after all, everyone has a stake in language variation. In the following paragraphs, we'll outline some of the aspects of language variation that teachers need to understand and operationalize.

▓ MULTILINGUALISM

The quotation which introduces this chapter reminds us that 'English' has a global role that has little to do with the nation that lends its name to this world language. English, for many people, might mean American English or English learnt as 'an additional language' (often known as EAL), or the lingua franca of business and computer technology. The international dimension of English puts particular responsibilities on English teachers to ensure that the 'texts' they use (every message communicated in a classroom) and the values they adopt avoid what Holliday (2000) has described as 'linguistic parochialism'. Holliday defines such parochialism as 'a state of mind in which a particular language is thought of as characterising and belonging to a particular people or nation' (2000: 131). If you are a first-language Welsh speaker you will fully appreciate how this Anglo-centric pressure works in the UK; if, however, you are a Welsh citizen but an English-only speaker you may well have felt linguistically excluded in certain cultural and social settings where the Welsh language is privileged. The past fifty years in the UK have added the global dimension to this powerful nexus of language interests, and every English secondary classroom will have links to this phenomenon. It is vital that English teachers embrace the pluralism of 'English'. Given the high profile of English as a global phenomenon, anything less than explicit positive engagement with this version of English amounts to a covert racism or colonialism. (Recall the 'language charter' introduced earlier in this chapter.)

How does this translate into classroom practice?

1. A rewarding, and perhaps essential, early project with any new class is to complete a languages map or inventory which traces the 'language resources' available to the group. This would embrace both pupil and family multilingualism, as well as regional dialects, and give appropriate status and visibility to the cultural resource which languages signal. (As a trainee teacher you might need to consult with mentors concerning any pupil sensitivities about placing home languages in the public domain.)
2. Language study will make explicit use of texts that reflect the international audience for English; this will include international literature as well as non-fiction, mass media and electronic media illustrations of the global interest in English beyond the literary canon.
3. Languages other than English would be heard in the classroom. Teachers would encourage first language usage in appropriate classroom settings. For example, small group planning or individual note-taking might be conducted in the pupil's first language if that aids fluency in thinking. More experienced bilingual pupils might 'code-switch' if other languages are available within a group, both to support other learners and to increase their own language repertoires. Just imagine how coaching instructions might be disseminated in the training sessions of many UK Premiership football clubs!

(There are powerful arguments, based on Vygotskian and neo-Vygotskian theories,[1] which locate language use at the centre of effective learning. The notion of language as a crucial learning tool should prompt teachers to encourage first language use where an activity serves a cognitive rather than a presentational purpose.)

▓ STANDARD ENGLISH

Within a multilingual frame of reference, the teaching of Standard English becomes a significant second order concern. It is a controversial and emotive topic, and English teachers need to be secure in their understanding of the concept and clear in their classroom applications. Cox (1991: ch. 3) provides an excellent starting point for all English teachers. 'Standard' is so easily misrepresented as 'correct' or 'proper' or even 'good', and influential media and pressure groups will readily exploit any slippage in meanings. We need to be clear about our terms of reference.

> Standard English is the 'prestige' variety of English that carries the agreed conventions and rules for almost all writing and public or formal communication. It is the version of English that has been codified for dictionaries and grammars, and has consequently high status as an international phenomenon. For these reasons, it is vital that all pupils learn to write and speak in Standard English – to enhance rather than to replace local language repertoires and dialects.

That said, there are further important distinctions to be drawn. Standard spoken English and standard written English are not the same phenomenon (more of that in the next section); standard spoken English comes with any regional accent; standard English is subject to change over time like any other language phenomenon. There is in fact more flexibility and variety in the concept of standard English than we might at first think; and globalization and electronic communication will continue to reshape the conventions of standard English. There are in fact relatively few non-standard forms in circulation in the UK – it is the frequency of their usage that might exasperate the teacher. For example, 'we was', 'them others/them teachers', 'should of', 'I didn't know nothing' will be recognized by most teachers as ingrained habits of both speech and writing.

These examples point to the sensitive links between language usage and identity. On the one hand, teachers must avoid giving pupils the impression that their patterns of speech are inferior or undesirable; but, on the other hand, they do pupils a disservice if they do not alert them to the power of standard English on the world stage. *English for Ages 5 to 16* (DES,1989), the original template for the National Curriculum, explored the rationale for teaching standard English in considerable detail and wisely advocated that teachers first introduce pupils to standard English through their writing, before modelling situations where standard spoken

English would be the norm (see Cox, 1991: ch. 3). This counsel still holds good; most English teachers will tell you how surprisingly effective their pupils can be when asked to role-play two professional adults in conflict, such as the headteacher and an 'offending' teacher or frustrated parent!

■ SPOKEN AND WRITTEN ENGLISH

> Pupils should be taught to use the vocabulary, structures and grammar of spoken standard English fluently and accurately in informal and formal situations.
>
> (DfEE, 1999, En 1 [5])

This presents a considerable challenge to teachers of English who attempt to 'standardize' pupils' *informal* language usage. Consider how you would feel if the mentors on your course began to monitor interactions with your fellow trainees in staffroom discussion. There are important differences between spoken and written standard English which the NC injunction quoted above seems to ignore.

First, there is little research done on spoken standard English and, consequently, there is considerable prejudice about its workings. Carter (1997: ch. 4) notes some of the commonly occurring grammatical features found in speech that will not appear in any grammar of English, based invariably on formal written examples. Transcribe a sequence from a radio or television discussion programme and you will find these features used as 'markers' to facilitate face-to-face communication: they include monitoring features such as 'you know' and 'like'; repetitions, back-tracking and grammatical mixing of tense or subject agreement to ensure the message is getting across. See how this works in this imagined political speech:

> We believe people are ready to make these difficult decisions we know how hard people work how much they expect from public services and yes we say they are ready to go that extra mile with us and yes we risk being unpopular but there's no way we are going to duck our responsibilities to the nation believe us on that.

This is actually quite colloquial, repetitive and grammatically overloaded, yet political speech-making would be classed as a 'formal speech situation' in NC terms. In practice, we would not notice these features of the discourse because it works within the conventions for rhetorical speech. It is not inferior to a written speech on the same topic – just different. So, when teaching pupils about spoken and written standard English, teachers need to present examples which help them appreciate the many varieties of

English usage and, most importantly, to help pupils realize that language use should take account of purpose and situation. Drama and role-play will clearly help pupils appreciate these subtleties where teacher correction or insistence on 'a standard' would only meet with resistance.

A second area of knowledge for teachers of English relates to the development of literacy in young learners (see Carter, 1990: ch. 13). For very young children, writing develops from the oral repertoire available to them – their writing will look rather like a transcription of their speech or the words of significant adults in their lives. From about the age of 8, teachers will detect the influence of reading (either teacher reading aloud or personal reading), as children's writing begins to take on a distinct form, adopting constructions more typical of written English. This process has begun when a child begins a story with 'once upon a time' and concludes it with 'and they all lived happily ever after'. The process has reached some maturity when the pupil writes; 'the first point I want to make is … and to conclude I would say that … '. This is, of course, a complex and uneven process, characterized by awkwardness, uncertainty and messiness as children try out new constructions. Reading experiences make a huge difference, producing enormous differentials in the 'oral/literate continuum' (Tannen, 1986) which secondary teachers need to be alert to throughout KS3 and KS4. A sympathetic understanding of the overlaps and continuities between spoken and written English is essential if teachers are to respond to pupils' writing in ways which encourage further experimentation – even when the experiment has not quite worked.

PLANNING TO TEACH ABOUT LANGUAGE

After this long but important journey of reflection, let us come back to practical matters. We present here a lesson plan for a language lesson, one produced by a trainee, Rachael, for use during her second placement (her medium-term planning for this unit of work is provided in Figure 2.3). Note how she has linked her objectives to the Framework for KS3.

ENGLISH LESSON PLAN

TOPIC: Language and Register   **DATE:** 22/3/02
YEAR/ABILITY GROUP: Year 9 – Low   **DURATION:** 70 mins.
TEACHING OBJECTIVES
All pupils should be able to:

1. Explore differing attitudes to language and identify characteristics of standard English that make it the dominant mode of public communication. (Sn10)

2. Use a range of drama techniques, including work in role, to explore issues, ideas and meanings, e.g., by changing perspectives. (SL12)

More able pupils should be able to:

3. Review and extend their own strategies for locating, appraising and extracting relevant information. (R1)

TEACHING AND LEARNING ACTIVITIES

Teaching Activity	Approx. Time	Learning Activity	Approx. Time
Starter: brainstorm key words from previous lesson. Explain objective: to understand about register and the use of standard English	5 mins	Pupils in pairs encouraged to add their key words to w/b. Pupils complete brief written description of SE from board notes	5 mins
Watch video extract of *News at Ten*	4 mins	Brief Q and A on the features of language evident in the extract	3 mins
Provide transcript and display OHP table for pupils to complete features of standard English: teacher modelling the task	10 mins	Pupils copy and complete table	15 mins
Explain 2nd task: to carry out brief role-plays to investigate the way that we speak in different situations (T. provides scenarios to include 1 informal and 1 formal situation)	3 mins	In pairs pupils carry out role-plays	10 mins
Ask to watch 1 or 2 of each role plays		Pupils perform their role-plays	5 mins
Plenary – learning outcome grid provided on OHT – pupils asked to say what they discovered about language use from role plays	10 mins		

Supplementary Support: Use of part-completed tables to support less able students' learning. Series of short tasks to maintain pace.

> Referring also to the 'at-a-glance' (medium-term) plan in Figure 2.3 and to your copy of the NC for English, list the areas of language study that this topic is likely to address.

CONCLUSION

Language study offers immense potential to the English teacher. We have tried in this chapter to give you some practical ideas about how to tap into this potential so that language investigation and analysis can be enjoyed by pupils as worthwhile areas of study alongside literature. To make this enjoyment possible, teachers need to feel engaged, curious and reasonably confident about language issues. This is a long-term professional commitment but we have tried to start this process by providing coherent models for language study, examples of language work in secondary classrooms, a language audit to help you record relevant knowledge, and a fuller discussion of some of the central concerns relating to language use in English classrooms. We hope you enjoy journeying with language in your own classrooms.

NOTE

1 For an introduction to Vygotskian theory, as it relates to teaching, see Mercer (1995).

SUGGESTED READING TO SUPPORT YOUR DEVELOPMENT

Bearne, E. (ed.) (1999) *Use of Language across the Secondary Curriculum.* London: Routledge.

Carter, R. (1997) *Investigating English Discourse: Language, Literacy & Literature.* London: Routledge.

Davison, J. and Moss, J. (eds) (2000) *Issues in English Teaching* (chs 6–9). London: Routledge.

	WEEK 1	WEEK 2	WEEK 3	WEEK 4	Evolving/changing ideas
Content	• A brief history of English	• Attitudes to accent/dialect • What is standard English?	• Contextualizing language	• The changing meanings of words	• Extend unit by looking at particular genres of writing, e.g., travel writing
Teaching and learning activities	• Extracts of language through history • Pupils construct a time line	• Excerpt from video to draw out elements of standard English • Watch video excerpt on accent and dialect • Pupils record snippets of conversation at home, on television etc. and analyse	• Extract from novel – how one character can alter their accent according to context • Role-play – how we speak in different contexts	• Call My Bluff – pupils identify the correct derivation for a modern word	
Resources	• *Cambridge Encyclopedia of The English Language* • *The Language Book Text*	• Looking at Language Text book • Video and audio excerpts	• *Northern Lights* by Phillip Pullman • Role-play character cards	• Looking at Language Text book • *Frantic Semantics and More Frantic Semantics*	
Assessment points (might not be necessary each week)		• Pupils write review of television programme in dialect • Departmental video on accent and dialect			• Pupils create piece of travel writing

2.3 AT-A-GLANCE UNIT PLAN

CHAPTER THREE

Investigating Grammar

[K]nowing more about grammar as part of knowledge about language, is to be empowered to respond to and to use grammar as central to the creation of textual meanings.

(Carter, 1997: 35)

INTRODUCTION

In the UK, grammar gets a bad press – sometimes literally. In a fascinating chapter charting the emotional potency of grammar as a disputed area, Cameron (1995: ch. 3) records the strident voices from the tabloid press, from politicians and even from the Prince of Wales, that have over the past twenty years claimed an interest in what she dubbed 'the grammar crusade'. In the rhetoric of this period, grammar was linked to discipline, to moral character, even to national standards of conduct. The passion or, more accurately, the prejudice is deep seated. An influential national report on English teaching published in 1921, The Newbolt Report, has this to say about pupils' standards of speech:

> The great difficulty of Elementary schools in many districts is that they have to fight against the powerful influences of evil habits of speech contracted in home and street. The teachers' struggle is thus not with ignorance but with a perverted power.
>
> (Newbolt, 1921, cited in Cameron, 1995: 96)

So grammar certainly packs a punch! Our aim in this chapter is to persuade you that grammar is a significant and fascinating area of English teaching, not a threatening minefield. As in the previous chapter, we want to encourage you to develop your *interest* alongside your knowledge of grammar, to help you sustain a curiosity about the workings of language whilst also learning more about the appropriate terminology.

Naming parts of speech is not the aim of grammar teaching; but knowing enough about the function of verbs in a sentence is a valid objective. Jokes, advertising and storytelling play with our implicit knowledge of grammar to create special effects and this provides fertile ground for English teachers. Consider this old joke:

> I was walking down the street one day and I met a guy who had a dog on a lead.
> 'Does your dog bite?' I said.
> 'No,' he said.
> So I bent down and stroked the dog. It bit my hand right on the knuckle there.
> 'I thought you said your dog doesn't bite,' I said.
> 'It's not my dog,' he said.
>
> (QCA, 1999a: 15)

The 'joke' depends on implicit assumptions about language use that the dog-minder chooses to ignore. Technically, the first speaker should have said 'does this dog bite?' rather than 'does your dog bite?' It is not essential that you know that *this* operates as a demonstrative adjective and that *your* operates as a possessive adjective in these sentences, but you can be sure that pupils (and adults too) will be more interested in learning about terminology when they are presented with authentic or amusing texts. And with only twenty-six letters in the English alphabet and some half a million words, we are bound to find text samples which amuse, confuse and infuriate.

Do not assume that terminology is the passport to good grammar teaching. Any experienced English teacher will tell you that if you teach the definition of a noun, the pupils will soon find a word that does not fit the definition. There is a delightfully mischievous poem by Michael Rosen 'Naming of Parts' that warns you against this approach. Instead, keep purpose and function to the fore. Look at complete texts (not sentences in grammar books) and consider what is worth analysing. If your pupils need to vary the way they use adjectives, then study a piece of advertising copy and invite the class to underline the adjectives with you. They might find adjectives used in multiples or adjectives at the start of a sentence and could model these findings in their own writing.

We hope you will want to learn more about the technical grammatical terms through your professional encounters with language in order to deepen you own understanding. During your training and beyond, you will need a good grammar manual as a reference point to help you (for example, Crystal, 1996; Keith, 1994); you will also find a useful glossary of terms in QCA's (1999b) *Improving Writing at Key Stages 3 and 4*. But keep curiosity, relevance and empowerment as guiding principles for your grammar investigations, and for your work with your own classes. Many pupils will find language analysis, if done imaginatively, at least as interesting as literature study. You have only to look at the popularity of A level English Language courses to know this. And do not feel you have to be a walking encyclopedia of grammatical terms to awaken this interest in the workings of language.

GRAMMAR AND THE ENGLISH TEACHER: SOME KEY CONSIDERATIONS

WHAT IS GRAMMAR?

First, let us establish a working definition of grammar appropriate to the teaching of English in the twenty-first century. (For a very succinct and interesting historical perspective on grammar, see Paper 1 in *The Grammar Papers*, QCA, 1998.) Essentially, the term 'grammar' describes the way language is organized to convey meaning up to sentence level and beyond at text level. If you recall the two approaches to language study in the previous chapter, grammar teaching would fit the second approach of close linguistic analysis. There are five levels of grammar within the organization of a sentence starting from the smallest meaningful unit: morpheme, word, phrase, clause, sentence. At text level, the term 'cohesion' is used to show how sentences are linked or organized to make meaningful coherent texts.

All these terms are used within National Curriculum English; children in Key Stages 1 and 2 are learning about morphemes when they study prefixes and suffixes. So, although you might already be feeling anxious about the label 'morpheme', remember that you have years of applied knowledge and experience with morphemes! The pedagogic question, which centres on when and how you introduce pupils to the terminology, will be discussed later.

Most grammar teaching in schools has historically focused on sentence-level grammar, using grammar exercises and drills with 'model' sentences that required pupils to identify nouns, prepositions etc. in replica sentences. Such teaching gave grammar its bad name. It became an elaborate labelling exercise deploying artificial and simplified sentences divorced from users' purposes; at worst such teaching undermined users' confidence in their own language. In reaction to this trend, the LINC project at the end of the 1980s proposed a new style grammar teaching (Carter, 1990; 1997) based on whole spoken or written texts relevant to other classroom purposes, perhaps by studying classroom literature, pupils' own writing or the everyday media texts influencing pupils' lives. This is the approach which we continue to advocate in this book, maintaining our faith in 'the text' as the cohering principle in English teaching.

The issue of relevance is particularly important. The traditional grammar teaching outlined above was premised on the belief that pupils' own writing would be improved by close analysis of sentence grammar. Research, however, found no clear links between such grammar teaching and improved writing performance (see Paper 6 in *The Grammar Papers*, QCA, 1998). The approach advocated by LINC and further developed by the QCA seeks to find a middle way that secures the role of grammar teaching in the general development of pupils' literacy and their appreciation of language:

> practice in writing, combined with a language focus which routinely draws attention to language features, patterns, choices and effects is more likely to improve pupils' grammatical range and competence than traditional, formal grammar teaching that makes no connection with pupils' language use.
>
> **(QCA, 1998: 48)**

Myhill (in QCA, 1999a: 10) makes the further point that English teachers do explicitly teach pupils the technical language of literary criticism (metaphor, alliteration, etc.) and should be similarly prepared to equip pupils to appreciate how the grammatical features of any text contribute to its meanings.

■ WHY GRAMMAR?

Keith proposes a significant role for grammar in our cognitive functioning which teachers need to consider very seriously:

> [T]here can be no doubt that a view of language in terms of how time (e.g. verb tenses and adverbs), space (e.g. prepositions and adverbs) and relationships (e.g. pronouns) are mapped out in the mind, is a matter of fundamental importance to our understanding of the ways in which we think.
>
> **(Keith, 1990, in Carter, 1990: 70)**

Consider the intellectual operations involved when you link clauses with conjunctions like 'however', 'until', 'therefore' or adverbs like 'consequently'. The grammatical selections we make are indicative of our cognitive map, and this link will be significant when we discuss children's writing development and the needs of pupils learning English as an additional language (EAL) in a later section.

Once we have the linguistic capacity to *choose* the way we organize words, then grammar becomes an aspect of individual speech and writing style. Older pupils respond well to the idea that grammar choices can help them establish a writing identity; grammar then becomes a resource rather than a curse. Understanding the available linguistic options and being able to analyse the effects created by others are surely items in the metalinguistic tool kit we would want all pupils to have. The effects of grammar choices can also be sinister. Many have commented on the use of the passive voice by media and government sources to conceal responsibility (see Cameron, 1995; Stubbs, 1990). Consider the following options:

The United States bombed Iraq last night

and

Iraq was bombed last night.

You can relate this to the outer layers of Figure 2.2 in the previous chapter; the grammar choices we make are influenced by political, cultural and social values. So, grammar can carry a heavy punch, and we owe it to our pupils to ensure that they understand how language can be manipulated to good and bad ends.

GRAMMAR IN THE NATIONAL CURRICULUM: ENGLISH

The introduction of *The National Literacy Strategy* (NLS) in primary schools (DfEE, 1998) and subsequently in secondary English classrooms as the *Framework for Teaching English: Years 7, 8 and 9* (DfEE, 2001b) has brought a new momentum to grammar teaching. Both documents, as noted in the previous chapter, are structured to provide teaching objectives based on word-level, sentence-level and text-level language analysis. The Framework is designed to make year-by-year progression in English easier to chart, with Key Objectives identified in boldface for each year group.

> Look again at the Framework and, for each year group, identify those objectives that you think would require close grammatical analysis of the kind we have identified above, listing them as word-, sentence- or text-level objectives. Mark any Key Objectives with [KO]. Now look at The National Literacy Strategy and see whether objectives for Years 5 and 6 provide a foundation for those you have already listed (there is a useful overview in section 3 of the National Literacy Strategy file).

The National Literacy Strategy for primary and secondary English consti-tutes a radical initiative that has the potential to transform pupils' knowl-edge about language. Primary teachers have been working with the NLS since 1998, so many pupils coming up to secondary schools should have some grasp of grammatical terminology, from vowel and syllable to com-pound and complex sentences. Knowledge of terminology does not of course, guarantee that pupils can write fluently in complex sentences, but secondary English teachers will need to be attuned to learners' prior expe-riences when planning for grammar teaching.

GRAMMAR TEACHING IN ENGLISH CLASSROOMS

As in the previous chapter, we will first provide some exemplar lesson ideas before considering an appropriate methodology for grammar teaching. Allowing for ability levels and previous experience, these activities can be used throughout Key Stages 3 and 4. We have also used them successfully with KS2 and A level students. All activities are intended as collaborative, interactive and investigative processes to stimulate curiosity about language rather than exercises in correctness or error detection.

• *Synonymous verbs*

Take a page of Dickens' prose and invite pupils to underline all the verbs used as alternatives to 'said'.

• *Concrete nouns and abstract nouns*

Investigate the distribution of abstract and concrete nouns in two extracts from different genres, e.g., a science manual and a travel brochure. Draw some conclusions.

• *The exquisite corpse (variants of)*

Teacher provides a model sentence on the board and lists the parts of speech being used:

Tall children ran rapidly   down   the   long, sleepy, silent streets.

Adj. Noun Verb Adverb Preposition Def. Article Adj. string   Noun

You can make this more or less difficult, but the game then operates like a game of consequences. Pupils are encouraged to make appropriate but adventurous vocabulary choices.

• *Simple and complex sentences*

Teacher provides two simple sentences and shows how they might be adapted and combined to make a complex sentence, then invites pairs to list as many alternative combinations as possible, without using *and* or *but*, eg:

> 1. The beaches were deserted at noon.
>
> 2. The sun shone directly over the horizon.

The teacher can then select pupils to provide the starting sentences. Pupils can also be invited to identify a writer's use of simple and complex sentences in a familiar sample of prose.

• *Phrases*

Pupils are asked to collect 20 television programme titles or book titles with more than one word in the title. They then categorize them as phrases (without a verb), e.g., *The Simpsons* or clauses/sentences (with verb), e.g., *Who Wants to be a Millionaire?*

• *Word classes*

Distribute words on cards that can fit into more than one class, e.g., bite (noun and verb), round (preposition, noun) and invite groups to classify them and then make sentences showing their various usages.

• *Language and power*

Pupils are invited to write the dialogue between a pupil and teacher, where the pupil is in trouble and the teacher in control. Class compare pupil/teacher language choices using given criteria, e.g., sentence type (command, question, statement), pronoun use, length of utterance, concrete/abstract nouns and draw conclusions about language choice and power.

Of course, all these grammar activities, enjoyable as they demonstrably are, can be just as ineffective in influencing pupils' personal language practices as more traditional exercises. To avoid a kind of tokenism where grammar becomes a cheery but distracting game, it is necessary to think about the way language issues are customarily addressed in your classroom. It is time to think about the methodology you adopt in order to create a culture of respect for language and a self-confidence amongst pupils as language 'detectives' and language users. If the climate is right, then the kind of investigative work listed above is likely to impact on learners' own practices.

■ ESTABLISHING THE CLIMATE

To achieve this climate, George Keith proposes that teachers encourage the practice of 'noticing' (cited in QCA, 1999a: 23). He suggests that teachers routinely note and share with pupils their observations about the working of language in any relevant classroom texts, from computer manuals and television advertisements to school rules and 'letters to parents', as well as the more predictable literary and non-literary texts used in English classrooms. If the teacher is able to stimulate curiosity about grammar by pointing to its everyday applications, then pupils are more likely to become relaxed but interested 'language observers' in their daily life. You might well find that pupils bring to class their own 'grammar samples' – perhaps an estate agent's leaflet or a piece of junk mail from the breakfast table.

This accumulation of casual observation, Keith argues, can result in a substantial knowledge base in language; and teachers can more comfortably find their way through small-scale investigation to establish a more robust theory of grammar.

> Functional and structural features noticed in a text can lead to a theoretical point of view in much the same way that successive journeys through a landscape inevitably lead to the construction of a map in the mind. Today, many teachers have to learn or rediscover grammar as they teach it, making the journey, noticing the features and constructing the map at the same time.
>
> (QCA, 1999a: 23)

■ THE GRAMMAR MAP

English grammar clearly requires a complex map, but English teachers have to face the challenge of becoming familiar with the landscape without overwhelming themselves and their pupils with the detail. Too often, the simple response has been to take a linear route, teaching nouns in Year 7, verbs in Year 8, etc. Rather than simplifying, this approach is more likely to deaden response to the dynamic operation of language. We do not learn our home languages in this linear fashion and, consequently, we need to find ways of teaching that acknowledge and celebrate the complex patterns of grammar deployed by all first-language speakers – in primary and secondary classes.

Working within the KS3 Framework, a first task with any new class would be to plot the existing grammar map to see which areas pupils have already 'visited'. Children who have been taught through the Strategy since its inception should have been introduced to all the terminology that even English teachers trained in the grammar tradition would have expected to teach during the whole of the 11–16 phase! (Look again at *The National*

Literacy Strategy, DfEE, 1998: 69–72.) This presents a curious and novel challenge for secondary trainee English teachers. There is not yet much research on the impact of NLS teaching in secondary English departments, but the noun/verb linear approach will certainly be an inadequate response when teaching Year 7 pupils with this kind of primary school background. The Framework for Key Stage 3 English assumes a level of knowledge (on the part of teacher and learner) that has already required many English departments to rethink their teaching of grammar.

> During school observations/placements, try to identify the strands of grammar teaching in departmental schemes of work. Discuss with departmental colleagues whether their schemes of work were modified to take account of *The National Literacy Strategy* in primary schools.

Given this background, a better starting point for grammar teaching is to work inductively through given texts, probing pupils' understanding of terminology as you observe the choices made by writers for particular effects and asking pupils to experiment with these features in their own writing. (There is an excellent example of this approach in *Not Whether but How* [QCA, 1999a: 23–7], as George Keith shows how the opening of Dick King-Smith's *The Sheep Pig* can be more fully appreciated through a study of the author's grammatical choices.)

In the same chapter, Keith offers a practical and principled grammar map to help English teachers present grammar more systematically (QCA, 1999a: 30–2. See also Keith, 1997; Keith and Shuttleworth, 1997). He suggests mapping grammar according to three main word classes:

- *Nouns* – grouped with adjectives, pronouns and determiners to make phrases.
- *Connectives* – conjunctions and prepositions. Keith describes these as some 200 crucial words that fasten together the remaining half a million words in modern English 'that make possible joined-up thinking'.
- *Verbs* – grouped with adverbs to make clauses and sentences (QCA, 1999a: 31).

This classification provides some simplification and a coherent overview, whilst retaining the essential dynamic of sentence grammar. Meaning-making, the creation of clauses and sentences, is the rationale for the map. Nouns make phrases, they name and label things, but verbs are the drive belts that provide sentences – and the action in the world. As in the following:

Gandalf the mighty wizard

Gandalf's wizardry saved Middle Earth

Keith's account of grammar is fascinating because it takes us beyond the naming of parts and invites us to see grammar like a working engine or a muscle, powering everything we do with language. The way that a learner uses connectives, for example, can provide teachers with clues about the child's writing development. We will consider this later in the chapter.

PLANNING TO TEACH GRAMMAR

As in the previous chapter, we provide below a sample lesson plan which focuses on the teaching of an aspect of grammar. This is just one lesson in a four-week unit intended to support pupils' ability to write to 'inform, explain and describe' (a National Curriculum requirement). The trainee teacher, Alexa, chose the device of a computer game that pupils would design, launch and then market. In a previous lesson, pupils had looked at the texts accompanying computer games (promotional material, introductions, instructions). Here pupils are using these models to write the introduction to their own game. Note how grammar is therefore seen as a layer within a rich seam of English experience, designed to achieve wider social ends – not as a discrete analytic exercise. This is in keeping with Keith's vision of grammar as a way of acting on the world, and with our vision of text at the centre of English – in this case, the production of texts by pupils.

(Sn1 refers to sentence-level objective 1 in the Framework, W1 refers to word-level objective 1 etc.)

ENGLISH LESSON PLAN
TOPIC: Introduction to computer game
YEAR/ABILITY GROUP: Yr 9   **DURATION**: 60 minutes
Middle/upper ability range
LEARNING OBJECTIVES
All pupils should be able to:
1. Use different ways of opening, developing linking and completing paragraphs. (Sn6)
2. Write with differing degrees of formality, relating vocabulary and grammar to context, e.g., using the active & passive voice. (Sn3)

More able pupils should be able to:

3. Recognize how lines of thought are developed and signposted through the use of connectives, e.g., nonetheless, moreover. (W8)

TEACHING AND LEARNING ACTIVITIES

Teaching Activity	Approx Time	Learning Activity	Approx Time
T. uses OHP to remind pupils of features of instructional writing. Ensure connectives and passive voice are noted in modelled text	10 mins	Pupils answer teacher questions, revising their previous learning	
T. supports round class. Selects one/two (not most able only) to 'show' in next phase of lesson		Pupils prepare first paragraph of their own introductions, focusing on 'hook' to interest audience in first sentence and varying the connectives used.	15 mins
T. uses OHT to model some of the good sentences, highlighting the features of language, e.g. formality of tone	10 mins		
		Pupils then plan, using a 'paragraph board' to draft the rest of their introductions. They list 5/6 connectives they'll try to incorporate	15 mins
T. uses w/ b to celebrate any interesting sentences/ clauses used by class, e.g. passive voice, effective connectives	10 mins	Pupils make additional notes during the plenary on their 'paragraph board'	

Differentiated support (e.g. your plans for SEN, EAL, etc.):
OHP modelling is designed to support less able. Groupings already selected to mix abilities sensitively. All exemplar material will be available for pupils to adapt.
ICT Use: End product will be completed in ICT suite – presentational aspects of introduction will be considered next lesson.
Assessment Opportunity: Informal observation of writing ability.
Resources: Samples of computer game promotional materials etc. Acetates/OHP pens.

GRAMMAR AND PUPILS' LEARNING

■ PUPILS' WRITING

An appreciation of the significance of grammar options can help teachers support their pupils' language development more effectively – and with the introduction of *Literacy across the Curriculum* (DfEE, 2001a) this applies to *all* secondary subject teachers. Understanding something about how grammar works helps us get to the deeper structures of our thinking processes. If learners use subordinated clauses in speech and writing, they are able to hold two propositions together and can privilege one over the other; if they use the passive voice they have learnt to conceal the subject under discussion. Adding to pupils' grammar options is therefore an important task for the English teacher.

In 1999, QCA published the results of the Technical Accuracy Project in *Improving Writing at Key Stages 3 and 4* (QCA, 1999b), providing detailed linguistic analyses of GCSE English writing, using categories such as sentence structure, noun and verb usage, to exemplify pupils' achievement at Grades F, C and A. Whilst the emphasis is on writing, the implications for the teaching of speaking and listening and reading are also evident. Some grammar choices lead to better writing and teachers can model these features in guided reading and reinforce them through role-play and other speaking and listening situations.

The raft of DfES literacy support materials produced for schools in the first years of the Framework (www.dfes.gov.uk/standards) has continued this trend for close linguistic analysis of pupil writing. Taking the Year 9 training materials as an example, pupils are taught how to construct longer sentences, focusing on connectives, opening and final phrases. They are invited to see how professional writers achieve textual cohesion. Samples of Year 9 writing are then analysed for simple/complex sentences, connectives and vocabulary choices. So, intending teachers will be expected to have this kind of grammatical vocabulary to join the departmental discussion about how to support pupil progress in English.

Taken together, this library of materials is an excellent example of grammar in action; the analysis is more concerned with how the whole text is organized, with the grammatical resources chosen by the candidate to make sense between clauses and across paragraphs, than with sentence-by-sentence detection of error. Carter makes a compelling argument for this kind of 'discourse grammar'.

> While not denying the importance of spelling, punctuation and certain core
> grammatical rules, quality in writing and in formal contexts of speaking can
> be demonstrated to belong much more within the rhetorical domains of
> cohesion and of signalling, structuring and sequencing information between
> and across clauses as well as the ability to manipulate grammatical resources
> at the level of complete texts and different genres.
>
> (Carter, 1997: 96)

Although Carter's words predate the current National Curriculum, it all
falls within the remit of the *Framework for Teaching English* at Key Stage 3.

■ GRAMMAR AND EAL DEVELOPMENT

A full review of appropriate pedagogy for EAL teaching is beyond the scope
of this chapter, but teachers need sufficient linguistic knowledge to appreciate that mastery of subject content might be concealed in the struggle to
communicate ideas in an additional language. This is not an issue about
teachers simplifying grammar choices but about being more aware of how
meanings are embedded in the grammar of spoken and written texts.
Indeed, teachers will need to target specialist vocabulary and sentence construction, providing explicit support in acquiring new grammar options
(the use of the passive voice in scientific reports is a classic example). If you
think of your experiences in learning a second language, the informal colloquial uses of language are often more difficult to absorb than precise,
specialist terminology, particularly if you have an interest in a particular
field.

So English teachers should not avoid formal and technical language usage,
but should ensure that it is taught explicitly, with opportunity for repetition and rehearsal in structured sequences. Misunderstanding and mis-
comprehension are most likely to occur when teachers are asking EAL
pupils to explain verbally or to read 'silently' for understanding. (This also
applies to many 'struggling' monolingual pupils and EAL pedagogies are
almost always good strategies for all teaching.) Teachers should therefore
be aware of complexity in reading material and devise ways of highlighting
particular grammatical constructions, such as complex sentences with
embedded clauses. In 2002, the DfES produced a significant library of practical materials, including video material, to help English teachers understand the language needs of EAL pupils. *Grammar for Writing: Supporting
Pupils Learning EAL* (DfES, 2002b, and available on the DfES website) follows the same trend noted above, offering grammatical analyses of samples
of EAL pupils' writing with many practical suggestions for support.

CONCLUSION

Our aim has been to present grammar as an intrinsically fascinating and a cognitively significant topic. The chapter has presented a rationale and a methodology for grammar teaching in English lessons, arguing for a purposeful study of grammar, using whole texts drawn from daily life to encourage pupils to use grammatical analysis to support their individual writing and speech development. We have defined the territory by locating grammar within the Framework for Key Stage 3 and National Curriculum English, seeking to provide both principled reasons and practical guidance for placing grammar at the heart of English teaching. Grammar choices help create 'the text', which we have proposed as the central motif in English teaching.

SUGGESTED READING TO SUPPORT YOUR DEVELOPMENT

Crystal, D. (1996) *Rediscover Grammar*. Harlow: Longman.

Keith, G. and Shuttleworth, J. (1997) *Living Language: Exploring Advanced Level English Language*. London: Hodder & Stoughton.

QCA (1999a) *Not Whether but How: Teaching Grammar in English at Key Stages 3 and 4*. London: QCA.

CHAPTER FOUR

Writing

Those who study the history of writing are convinced that it is one of the most momentous of human inventions … It makes us conscious of language itself in ways that affect both our public and private lives.

(Meek, 1991: 23)

Most writers in school live in the eternal present, with no feeling of growth. Writing is a daily duty like teeth-cleaning, not a long-term process of developing competence and control.

(National Writing Project, 1985–89)[1]

INTRODUCTION

These two quotations frame the central challenge in the writing curriculum: how to ensure pupils see writing as a vital tool to shape their lives, rather than an exercise in classroom conformity. If we think of oral communication, reading, and writing as the essential channels of human learning, schools have traditionally placed most emphasis on writing in the formal curriculum. It is worth asking why. Writing has a visibility that can be more readily monitored and quantified than reading or speech; it all too easily becomes a control mechanism – even a punishment. The second quotation from the findings of the National Writing Project (influential in shaping writing practices across all school phases and subjects in pre-national curriculum days) points to some of the darker consequences of the misuse of writing in schools. At the start of the twenty-first century, the Key Stage 3 Strategy is once again highlighting the need for a cross-curricular dynamic in the teaching of literacy. Its approach to writing owes much to the principles of the National Writing Project and this chapter will seek to identify best practice in the teaching of writing, using these two major initiatives as reference points.

CONDITIONS FOR WRITING

What are the growing conditions necessary for writing to flourish in the classroom? To put it starkly and provocatively, writing needs:

- reading
- a purpose
- an audience
- structure and form
- time and space to practise
- a teacher to model the craft of writing.

We will now look at each of these conditions in a little more detail.

READING

'Writing needs reading' was a mantra associated with Frank Smith, an influential American literacy guru of the 1980s. In other words, experienced writers borrow and adapt the voices, styles and ideas they pick up from their reading; they have models to draw on and do not feel the 'tyranny of the blank page' in the same way as many young writers in classrooms. Teachers who read to pupils from the rich diversity of fiction and non-fiction available to English teachers can encourage their pupils to experiment with form, style and voice in 'safe' surroundings. Reading, then, provides the models or the templates that make sustained and interesting writing possible, provided the teacher makes the potential links explicit.

PURPOSE AND AUDIENCE … TIME AND SPACE

The National Writing Project played a crucial part in first highlighting the significance of audience and purpose for young writers in schools. Across the UK, teachers involved in the project came to see how narrow the writing curriculum was. Children wrote because the teacher told them to, and often without clear guidance about format or genre; the only audience for most writing was the teacher who routinely acted as an assessor. Now consider what prompts you to write as an adult: shopping lists, social messages to family and friends, letters of complaint, diaries, emails, work reports, etc.

You write in many formats, with clear purposes and for many different audiences, varying tone and register accordingly. The National Curriculum of 1989, its subsequent revisions and the 2001 Framework for KS3 English have ensured that writing in different forms and for a variety of purposes is central to the writing curriculum.

Look at the 2001 Framework for KS3 English: Writing. You will see that pupils need opportunities to write: *to imagine/explore/entertain; to inform/explain/describe; to persuade/argue/advise; to analyse/review/comment.*

Select one year group and one of these subsets. How many writing tasks can you devise to cover the text-level writing objectives? Ensure your pupils write in a variety of formats, e.g., an information leaflet to introduce beginners to text-messaging; the opening paragraphs for a romance novel, a ghost story or a horror story.

Teachers can make writing even more focused when they specify an audience other than themselves; this clearly helps pupils become more aware of style and register as they adjust their choice of format, vocabulary, sentence length, even punctuation, to suit the given audience. For example, a group project asking pupils to market their home town/city for their own age group and then for the 30–40-year-old client group should generate discussion and awareness of language choices in ways that add to pupils' confidence and enjoyment in language. (You should see overlaps here with the kind of language study advocated in Chapter 2.)

This example also underlines two other factors in good writing practices: the possibility of collaboration in writing and the need for sustained time. Consider another description drawn from National Writing Project findings and compare this with your own school experiences: 'most writing in schools is done in solitary confinement. The writer, imprisoned in the task, seeks release in the perfunctory and the minimum'. We have to do all we can to ensure that this dismal image is a thing of the past. Allowing pupils to work in pairs and small groups on extended writing projects can be liberating for pupils and rewarding for teachers – peers can act as guide, mentor and even assessor for each other's writing, creating another 'safe haven' for experimentation and consolidation.

The notion of 'extended writing' is also significant here. One of the unintended effects of the National Literacy Strategy in primary schools has been the neglect of sustained time provided for pupils to work at a piece of writing over time (see Frater, 2001). This has been acknowledged and the Framework for KS3 does not promote the much publicized 'literacy hour' as the centrepiece of literacy teaching. Training materials to support Framework teaching for Year 8 (DfES, 2002c) identify extended writing as a priority teaching objective and the following 'keynotes' of the writing curriculum: *experiment, craft, extend* and *control*. The upbeat message says: 'pupils at this age need to widen their repertoire, try on new voices, registers and text types. To gain stylistic control, they need time to play with language and test its limits' (DfES, 2002c: 24). This confident, relaxed description is a far remove from the strict regime of the time-driven literacy hour. Teachers will welcome this shift of emphasis.

▧ STRUCTURE AND FORM

We referred earlier to 'the tyranny of the blank page', which engenders the equivalent of writer's block in the minds of many classroom writers. Desktop publishing packages now make it very easy for the teacher to avoid this trap, by providing visually attractive prompt-cards and worksheets to support the hesitant writer.

The teaching tool known as *the writing frame*, and widely used in the National Literacy Strategy/Key Stage 3 Strategy, is designed, in part, to relieve writer's block, by providing a structure for, specifically, non-fiction writing. Writing frames aim to lessen the cognitive 'load' as pupils engage with both content and the technical challenges of composition. Sentence starters are provided to help the novice writer work within the structure of a given genre. For example, to help a pupil sustain an argument the teacher might provide a worksheet with the following prompts:

> In this leaflet, I want to argue that
>
> My first reason is
>
> A further reason is
>
> However
>
> To conclude

(For further examples, see Lewis and Wray, 1997; Wray and Lewis, 1997.) Whilst such frames can be helpful for the unsure and inexperienced writer, they need to be used selectively and flexibly to avoid stifling individual style and creativity in writing.

Writing frames draw on the characteristics and conventions of different types of writing (the travel brochure, the information manual, the recipe book, the romance); and the teacher's understanding of the generic features of a given text should inform the production of any writing frame. These types of writing are often called genres, although the National Curriculum (DfEE, 1999: 38) refers to them as 'forms of writing'. The list of more than twenty forms of writing, from poems and playscripts to prospectuses and campaign literature, provides a rich and challenging curriculum for Key Stage 3 and 4. The Framework (DfEE, 2001b) gives flesh to this list, by identifying typical discursive features (at word, sentence and text level) for explicit teaching. The young child who begins a story with 'once upon a time' and the older pupil who prefaces a pamphlet with 'the reader might like to know' have already understood something about genre – it is for the skilled teacher, sensitive to the patterns of language, to place such features of language at the child's disposal through explicit teaching opportunities. (The KS3 Strategy *Literacy across the Curriculum* file has an excellent section titled 'Writing non-fiction' which explores the generic features of a range of texts [DfEE, 2001a, with accompanying video].)

You can also invite pupils to transgress generic boundaries in amusing ways that help make visible the generic features of writing. Skilled writers do this all the time. (Chapter 2 refers to the Ahlbergs' celebrated *Jolly Postman* and offers ideas for mixed genre story-writing.) Drama conventions such as role-play and hot-seating can encourage pupils to experiment with the less familiar conventions of interviews and public meetings before attempting to incorporate such features in their writing. And, of course, the more examples of generic style you provide from a wide range of written and media material, the more confident your pupils will become. A recent postgraduate trainee, Heather, had downloaded from www.movie.com an extract from the film *A Few Good Men* to analyse the language features of a courtroom. Using the printed extract and video clips, she very effectively provided her pupils with 'a writing frame' to explore the generic features of advocacy or cross-examination. This would certainly meet the NC requirement that pupils write 'to persuade, argue and advise, focusing on presenting a case' (DfEE, 1999: 39).

▓ A TEACHER TO MODEL THE CRAFT OF WRITING

The National Literacy Strategy (DfEE, 1998) and its secondary counterpart, the Framework (DfEE, 2001b) have pioneered the development of guided writing and shared writing as features of good practice in English classrooms. Drawing from sound theoretical principles (see Beard, 2000), both strategies are designed to unpack the skills and behaviours of the experienced writer, casting the teacher as the articulate practitioner and mentor in the craft. (English training resources for the KS3 Literacy

Strategy provide good video examples of teachers using these processes.)

Shared writing requires the teacher to engage in the act of writing – in collaboration with the whole class – using OHP, flipchart or interactive whiteboard to show how any writer struggles to make decisions about such things as word choice, sentence order, sentence type and paragraph structure in the course of writing.

Guided writing follows from shared writing, as the teacher moves groups one step further towards independent writing by providing specific prompts (the writing frame would be one such prompt) to allow pupils to make connections from teacher modelling to a negotiated written outcome – often just a paragraph written to meet specific generic patterns.

Guided and shared writing activities are trying to access the deeper patterns involved in composition and are potentially very liberating. When teachers use examples of 'good' writing which they admire, and can enthusiastically explore the texture of a given text with a class (note the lexical connection between text and texture) and then illustrate these features through guided and shared writing, pupils are more likely to feel empowered to join the community of writers. Compare this possibility with the dismal description of writing as a chore presented earlier in the chapter and you might agree that these strategies should be part of a teacher's repertoire. They require the kind of confidence with language analysis addressed in chapters 2 and 3, an appreciation of the range of 'quality' texts available to teachers and the experience to recognize the potential of a given text to further pupils' appreciation of genre. These are tough challenges for the beginner teacher, but ones that we hope you will take up.

During school placements and observations, ideally in both primary and secondary settings, seek out the teachers who make use of guided and shared writing and observe their techniques. The National Strategy English department training materials provide a very helpful model to aid classroom observation (DfEE, 2001c: 41, and accompanying video).

LEARNING TO WRITE

CONNECTING THE SPOKEN AND THE WRITTEN WORD

If writing is indeed 'one of the most momentous of human inventions' (Meek, 1991: 23), teachers need to appreciate how each individual learner becomes a writer. As secondary teachers, you are likely to spend much time wishing your pupils were better writers; but it is both reassuring and educative to be reminded of how far all young writers have already travelled when they put pen to paper. Unlike speech, writing is not part of our 'natural' order. In the evolution of the human species over some 50,000 years, writing has emerged over the past 5,000 years (see Crystal, 1997). Literacy is not a universal expectation in all societies; a hundred years ago in the UK, there would be no expectation of anything beyond rudimentary literacy for the mass of the population. Compare this with national reading and writing expectations of the National Curriculum for all 5- to 16-year-olds and you will appreciate how much we are expecting of our pupils.

To appreciate something of the wonder of children's development as writers you should spend time with the nursery and reception teacher who first helps children to form letters and construct words. You will be amazed that these skilled professionals can 'read' their pupils scripts when you may see only marks, scribbles or symbols on the page. These same children will be writing stories, poems and descriptions before they leave KS1 classrooms – already a remarkable achievement. To understand something of how this development takes place we need to appreciate that beginner writers use the spoken language patterns they bring to school to construct their first sustained pieces of writing. In other words, they will write down what they have heard around them. Perera (1984) cites Kroll's helpful model for understanding writing development, showing how speech and writing are interlinked. Kroll proposes four phases: *preparation, consolidation, differentiation* and *integration.* In the first phase children are absorbed in the physical task of handwriting, and during the consolidation phase they begin to write what they can already say. Recall all those stories connected by 'and then' or 'but'. You will probably recognize, from your limited experience of secondary age writers, that many of the features of colloquial, everyday conversation are still very evident in their scripts.

Consider these two sentences. They illustrate something of the gulf between Kroll's consolidation and differentiation phases, and the real challenge for all teachers of English.

There was this monster and he was really scary and as big as a giant. The people in the hall were terrified and no one moved an inch they were that scared.
Once upon a time, a great monster entered the hall of the feasting men. A shadow of fear crept over the company – everyone sat frozen to the spot.

The differentiation phase is crucial because it marks the point at which writers borrow vocabulary, sentence patterns and textual organization from their experience of reading and hearing more formal spoken language. They become aware of choice and of style and, as a result, can begin to claim some authorial control over their writing. Perera describes this stage: 'there is often awkwardness as children try out new constructions, adopt forms they have met in their reading, and swerve erratically from over-formality to colloquialism and back again' (1984: 208). Whilst Kroll suggests this phase might begin at around 9 or 10 years of age, it seems likely that most secondary age pupils will be located somewhere within this 'experimental stage' during KS3 and often into KS4. It is therefore very important that English teachers can recognize both the significance of experimentation in children's writing and the influential role of the texts they provide as models for writing. (The integration phase is marked by the writer's confidence in deploying a range of styles to meet the demands of most written tasks.)

WRITING AND THINKING

The shift outlined above – from the influence of spoken to written language patterns – also involves a significant development in thinking. This has something to do with the different functions of the spoken and written word. Speakers are in a 'live' situation and can rely on gesture, intonation, awareness of audience reaction etc. to make sure they are understood. (The chances of miscommunication are increased if any of these factors are removed – phone conversations between friends are likely to require more communicative 'work' than face-to-face encounters.) But the writer has to overcome the barriers of time and space; without the reactions and expectations of the audience to guide and encourage, she/he has to anticipate the effects of their words on the imaginary reader. This requires a degree of abstract thinking, as well as considerable courage on the part of the young writer. Pupils who can write a set of instructions held together by cohesive ties like 'first, secondly' … etc. have learnt to organize their thoughts in important ways. Young writers who have learnt to structure their ideas in writing are apprenticed to a very powerful medium: they have access to more complex ideas, can extend their thinking, and enjoy the satisfaction that comes from creating an effect in a powerful medium – be it in narrative, persuasive or informative writing. (The word processor has added greatly to our capacity to use writing as a thinking tool, mirroring in its cut/paste and edit/delete facility the best practices of fluid, creative risk-taking minds.)

TEACHING WRITING IN THE NATIONAL CURRICULUM

WHERE ARE WE NOW?

Reviewing recent approaches to the teaching of writing, Myhill concludes that 'in spite of public concern over reading standards, it is writing which is the least well-managed aspect of the English curriculum' (2001: 12). National test results to 2002 have suggested that writing lags behind reading and therefore remains a key governmental priority; the NLS in primary schools seems to have had a significant impact on the effective teaching of reading, but has been less effective in raising standards in writing (see DfEE, 2000b). *Grammar for Writing* provides an interesting diagnosis of current writing pedagogy, before offering an 'NC model of writing' (DfEE, 2000b: 10–12). Its diagnosis of the average child's diet is all too familiar:

- Most writing is narrative.
- There is a high proportion of unfinished or poorly finished work.
- The teacher's corrections and comments have little effect.
- The child's writing does not seem to improve over time.

Prevailing models for writing are described as 'teaching by correction' where the teacher provides a stimulus for independent writing and then responds through discussion or marking. *Grammar for Writing* (DfEE, 2000) proposes instead 'teaching at the point of writing', involving the modelling by teachers of the decisions writers make in the process of com-position (see the earlier discussion of shared and guided writing). By adopting this approach, teachers are more likely to convince pupils that writing is not an automated linear process that adults manage effortlessly. If learners are to appreciate writing as a dynamic tool for learning and self-expression in the adult world, they need to realize how messy and provi-sional the writing process can be.

SO WHY ARE PUPILS 'NOT MAKING THE GRADE' IN THE WRITING CURRICULUM?

There is a delicate balance to achieve when teaching writing – between 'message' and 'mechanics'. Writers must want to communicate; the message should be the drive belt. But for many, adults as well as children, the frus-trations of transcribing their ideas onto the page overwhelm their best intentions. Writing becomes a spelling and punctuation exercise, with the expectation of error and teacher disapproval. A shrewd self-defence can emerge – write only what you feel technically safe with – and the result can be dull, unambitious written responses. National writing priorities for English departments, based on test results at KS2 and KS3, have confirmed this view (DfEE, 2001c: Introduction):

> more developed use of a range of sentence structures [subordinate clauses, expanded noun phrases]
>   better use of paragraphs to structure writing and improve coherence [conjuncts and adverbials to link sentences and paragraphs]
>   greater accuracy in spelling and punctuation.

It is, of course, easier to diagnose the problem than to remedy it. These priorities do not, in themselves, help the teacher balance 'message and mechanics'. Indeed, you might feel they only identify the very reasons why children fail to sustain a love of writing.

The National Literacy initiative, in both primary and secondary phases, was designed to provide teachers with the means to break this negative loop, and to retain the delicate balance noted above. In particular, the aim was to provide a more principled analysis of children's abilities and the classroom materials to intervene sensitively to raise achievement. As a result, English teachers are undoubtedly better informed about pupils' expected levels of achievement and have clearer writing priorities. The National Strategy has provided a library of highly focused and practical materials to support the identified priorities (go to www.dfes.gov.uk/keystage3), but these still depend crucially on the English teacher's capacity to foster the will to write. Arguably, the emphasis on sentence-level intervention might cause teachers to forget how important it is to have something to communicate (and *Grammar for Writing* [DfEE, 2000b] and *Improving Writing at Key Stages 3 and 4* [QCA, 1999b] perhaps encourage this tendency). Whilst on placement in English departments, you must judge for yourself whether English teachers continue to provide exciting contexts for writing whilst trying to attend to the compositional and technical aspects of writing.

WHAT IS AN APPROPRIATE WRITING CURRICULUM FOR AGES 11 TO 16?

Let us remind ourselves of the ambitious, exciting range of writing experiences enshrined in the NC for English. Use the list below and underline the writing 'forms' you have seen teachers encouraging pupils to use during your time in schools.

Reviews, commentaries, articles, reports

Polemical essays, letters to an editor, campaign literature, editorials, brochures

Memos, minutes, prospectuses, plans, records, summaries, information leaflets

Stories, diaries, poems, playscripts, autobiographies, screenplays

---

These are all taken from the National Curriculum for English (DfEE, 1999: 39) – currently the official curriculum – but we have reversed the order of presentation. If you ignore the final line in the box above, would you have many examples to underline? If your response is positive, then you have worked with teachers who are aware of concerns about a writing curriculum based only on fiction and narrative. Research has consistently found that boys engage more with school literacy practices if on-line technologies and factual/information texts are integrated in the reading/writing curriculum (see, for example, Daly, 2000; Millard, 2000). Ask yourself, too, which of the listed forms of writing you might find most helpful in your adult life. The Strategy has worked hard to address this familiar imbalance in the English writing curriculum, and publishers have also responded to the challenge of non-fiction.

Challenge yourself to think how you might introduce any one of the above listed 'forms of writing' to a less able group of pupils.

Example – Minutes
Prepare a brief version of a set of minutes from a staff meeting in a school like yours (persons anonymous of course, but choose an issue in which students might have a stake: pupils' behaviour outside school, school trips etc.).

Prepare a checklist of all the generic features and let pupils circle the items on the list as you read the minutes in a whole class setting, using an acetate to focus on specific features.

With the class, devise a list of issues for a staff/student council meeting. Assign roles and act out as formally as possible, using a video facility if available. Provide a writing frame using the features discussed above and ask pupils to devise a set of minutes, in pairs or individually.

Arguably, the central challenge for future teachers of writing is to ensure that they provide the broadest possible curriculum, sampling the rich store of non-fiction and making its conventions explicit for pupils to use as models. This theme is taken up in Strategy training materials for Years 8 and 9 and in the revised 2003 Key Stage 3 tests.

PLANNING FOR WRITING IN THE CLASSROOM

Now consider a lesson plan devised, as part of a much larger unit on instructional and informational writing.

ENGLISH LESSON PLAN

TOPIC: Informational writing: recipes for different audiences

YEAR/ABILITY GROUP: Yr 8 middle/upper ability range

DURATION: 70 minutes

LEARNING OBJECTIVES

All pupils should be able to:

1. Describe a process, using language with an appropriate degree of formality. (W 12) (also S&L 4)

2. Recognize how lines of thought are developed and signposted through the use of connectives e.g. next, finally. (W14)

More able pupils should be able to:

3. Experiment with different language choices to establish the tone of the piece (i.e. whether 'youth' or adult audience). (W7)

TEACHING AND LEARNING ACTIVITIES

Teaching Activity	Time	Learning Activity	Time
Starter: Television clip of Celebrity Chef with cooking instructions	5 mins	Pupils jot down any words that signal the stages of the process	
Whole class feedback: 5 mins. T. adds words to w/b – separate columns for connectives and verbs that instruct [imperatives] e.g. Connectives: *meanwhile* Verbs: *stir, mix, slice*			
		Pairs try to communicate the stages of the television recipe to each other, using 'signpost' words	10 mins

Teaching Activity	Time	Learning Activity	Time
		Same pairs given two contrasting recipes (e.g. Jamie Oliver and Delia Smith – BUT NOT REVEALING AUTHOR) They explore the two categories of words as above, making notes	15 mins
Whole class feedback T. uses OHT of recipes to draw out differences between the two styles, e.g., precise connectives, verb usage, 'trendy' word usage. Pupils invited to guess at author, using evidence	10 mins	Pupils make additional notes during the plenary to prepare them for writing their own recipes	
T. provides a set of ingredients (similar to those in sample recipes)		Pupils write into homework books Solo writing: Pupils begin to construct a recipe for a youth 'audience' or a more traditional 'audience'	5 mins 15 mins
Plenary T. reads sentences from one or two successful examples, to identify style featured through language choice	5 mins	Continue in next lesson	

DIFFERENTIATED SUPPORT (e.g. your plans for SEN, EAL etc.):
Modelling on OHP is designed to support less able. Pairings already selected to mix abilities sensitively. Most able will have to complete contrasting styles. Less able will choose their strongest 'style' to concentrate on ('Delia' style is an easier model).

ICT USE: End product will be completed in ICT suite – Jamie Oliver and Delia Smith website presentational values to be considered in future lessons

ASSESSMENT OPPORTUNITY: Informal observation of writing ability

RESOURCES: Recipes from Jamie Oliver and Delia Smith website – sample of recipe books if possible. Acetates/OHP pens

> Bearing in mind the features of good practice in the teaching of writing we have proposed in this chapter, try to identify some of the features of this lesson plan that might predict successful outcomes. Begin by reflecting on how the lesson tried to balance the creative and the technical aspects of writing.

THE ASSESSMENT OF WRITING

> Telling students that they need to 'try harder' is no better than telling a bad comedian that he needs to be funnier.
>
> **(Wiliam and Black, 2002: TES, 4 Oct)**

In this chapter we have aimed to provide suggestions for encouraging pupils to write in ways that consolidate and extend their existing repertoires. Skilled teachers of writing also know that teacher responses to children's writing can dramatically extend or, sadly, reduce pupils' effectiveness as writers. In this final section, we will touch briefly on this important topic to provide you with sufficient guidance to help you explore assessment more fully in schools.

Think back to your undergraduate writing. Consider how you felt when submitting important assignments. Do you remember whether tutors' feedback motivated or demotivated you – or simply left you 'in the dark'? The mixed feelings of vulnerability, hopefulness and uncertainty will be similar to those experienced by pupils in your classes – even if they have found ways of pretending otherwise. You also need to remember what we have already discussed about the multiple demands the young writer faces as soon as she/he begins to compose. When every sentence requires a decision about ideas, vocabulary, punctuation, spelling and text organization, teachers need to find a sensitive and generous tool for assessment. Without such a tool, it is too tempting to 'mark' surface features such as misspellings and to ignore 'deeper' features of text organization.

Using the following headings, devise an assessment pro forma that might be used by an English teacher to provide feedback on pupils' writing.

Aspects of Writing	For Example:
Organization	Openings, conclusions Linking sentences and paragraphs Cohesion of the whole text
Presentation	Handwriting, use of ICT Layout, appropriateness of format, e.g., use of graphic or other illustrative material
Ideas/content	Themes, ideas, vocabulary Sustained or original writing Sense of audience and fitness for purpose
Spelling and punctuation	Phonetic spelling Misspelling of 'regular' words Particular patterns, e.g., double letters, -ly endings Occasional misspelling of unfamiliar words Use of commas, full stops, apostrophes, capital letters, direct speech, etc.
Effort	

In devising this pro forma, you have several important questions to consider.

1. Does it matter whether you use grades and marks, as well as comments?
2. Is there a place for pupil self-assessment or peer assessment?
3. Is the response constructive and encouraging?
4. Have you provided practical and clear feedback that the child can use to improve next time?
5. Have you provided a mechanism to check whether the child has acted on your advice?

Extensive research by Wiliam and Black (1998; 2002) across a range of secondary classrooms has focused on these questions as central to the learning process. Controversially, they concluded that comments lead to better learning than grades or marks and, most startling of all, giving marks *and* comments leads to no improvement at all. This is because pupils will only look at marks and ignore any comments if this 'mixed economy' is used.

Marking takes a great deal of an English teacher's time and these findings suggest it is vital to think hard about the principles of assessment as a trainee teacher, before the unreflective habits of routine marking become the norm. You should be provoked by Wiliam and Black's observation:

> At present, a teacher will typically spend more time marking a student's work than the student will spend following it up – which suggests the teacher's time is less valuable! (Wiliam and Black, 2002: 8–9)

The kind of assessment implied in the questions above is often called formative assessment; it is intended to acknowledge the learner's individual needs and of course to provide the teacher with the professional information to support further learning. Wiliam and Black's research suggests that improvements in formative assessment can raise GCSE scores by more than half a grade, and provide teachers and pupils with an exciting joint learning project on the way! Arguably, the quality of formative assessment can make the difference between satisfactory and good or very good teaching – with all the rewards that can bring.

CONCLUSION

The electronic revolution of the twenty-first century should transform our reading and writing practices in ways as profound as the invention of the printing press. English departments should be shaping this agenda in creative ways. We hope that this chapter will provide you with some guiding principles and a little inspiration to help you ensure that classroom writing is never a clerical drudgery but a liberating investment in the future.

NOTE

The NWP (1985–1988) was a government-backed project, managed by the School Curriculum Development Committee and administered in its final year by the newly-formed National Curriculum Council.

SUGGESTED READING TO SUPPORT YOUR DEVELOPMENT

Millard, E. (2000) *Differently Literate: Boys, Girls and the Schooling of Literacy*. London: Falmer.

Myhill, D. (2001) *Better Writers*. Suffolk: Courseware Publications.

Qualifications and Curriculum Authority (1999b) *Improving Writing at Key Stages 3 and 4*. London: QCA.

CHAPTER FIVE

Reading and Literature

INTRODUCTION: WHAT IS READING?

Defining reading is no easy matter. We all think we know what we mean by 'reading', and yet there have been many fierce debates and disagreements over the years. Those debates, and the heat and light generated, are testimony to the educational and cultural importance of reading.

As secondary teachers of English and Literacy, we need to see ourselves as teachers of reading. That is a recent development; stereotypically, according to secondary teachers, pupils are taught to read in primary schools. In secondary schools, English teachers build on those skills, to give pupils access to a range of predominantly literary texts. However, recent developments in the requirements of the literacy curriculum have meant that secondary teachers are now more aware of their role in and responsibility for developing pupils in Key Stages 3 and 4 – and beyond – as readers. And that means developing reading skills systematically and deliberately. If we are to fulfil the requirement of the National Curriculum to enable our pupils to access a wide range of texts, then we have to address at the same time the issue of teaching our pupils to develop the necessary skills to cope with the range of diversity; reading a poem requires reading skills which are different from reading a train timetable.

Apart from those pupils who still need specialist teaching to enable them to acquire the necessary fundamental skills, there is scope for the secondary teacher to enable pupils to make progress as readers in a coherent and systematic way. Although we started this chapter by saying that a definition of reading is problematic, there are a number of interconnected elements that we intend to work with in this chapter:

- Reading is an active process.
- Reading is about making meaning(s) from texts.
- Reading is invariably purposeful, whether it be for pleasure, or to extract information;
- Reading takes place in a wide range of contexts.

In that way, we can be said to be defining reading.

In addition, we cannot talk about developing pupils as readers if we cannot indicate what progress looks like; if we have a model of progress in reading, we can also plan for appropriate developments, both for individuals and for whole classes.

But progress in reading is hard to define, and there is always a danger of oversimplifying what is a complex cognitive and cultural process. In addition, there is still no resolution of the top-down v. bottom-up debate. Those who subscribe to a predominantly 'bottom-up' view see reading development starting with the smallest units of language and moving through the gradations of letters and words and sentences and paragraphs towards whole texts. Those who prefer the 'top-down' view think that learners' first encounters with reading are with whole texts – whether they be picturebooks at bedtime or television programmes in the lounge or advertising posters in the street. Therefore, so the argument goes, we encourage pupils to tackle whole texts, and in that process teachers support them in engaging with the smaller units of those texts, but always in the context of the whole text.

Current practice seems to incorporate elements of both approaches. At a whole-text level, pupils ought to progress towards the skills of inferential reading (reading between the lines) and critical engagement. At the same time, investigation and understanding of language in texts at word and sentence level are expected to gain increasing complexity and sophistication, including the use of appropriate linguistic and textual terminology.

Progress, therefore, is defined in stages leading to the higher order skills of analysis and engagement. The pedagogic processes to support that development include:

- active engagement with texts – there will be more on that later in this chapter

- a recognition that reading is a social activity, involving the testing of interpretations through sharing them with others – the so-called 'reading community' view

- developing in readers a rule-governed view of texts – not rigidly so, but before pupils can experiment with breaking the rules they need to know what the rules are in the first place. This view connects with genre-informed views about teaching about texts

- providing pupils with opportunities to experience and engage with as wide a range of texts as possible, bearing in mind the inclusive use of the word 'text' in this book

- involving pupils in monitoring their achievements and progress – through reading logs, target-setting and recognition of significant successes.

This chapter goes on to consider the teaching of reading in the context of teaching literature. In many ways, such an approach goes against the grain of this book's view about 'text'. However, it is beyond the scope of this chapter to provide a fuller discussion of reading in its broadest conceptualization. (For a very focused and practical presentation of the range of issues for secondary teachers of reading, you would be well advised to read Dean [2000].)

Nevertheless, we hope that you can see how approaches and techniques advocated here for literary texts can be adapted for a wider range of texts, and we would encourage you to do that. For those of you teaching subjects in addition to or other than English, the strategies advocated later in this chapter lend themselves to uses across the curriculum – indeed, we would want you to draw on these pedagogic approaches whenever there is a focus on developing pupils' abilities to:

- make meaning(s) from texts

- extract appropriate information or follow the stages of an argument

- critically engage with the techniques and purposes of texts

- transform one text into another

- successfully create texts for particular readerships, listeners, or viewers

- make appropriate and imaginative choices from a range of texts for identified purposes in defined contexts.

LITERATURE AND READING

Any exploration of the role of literature in developing pupils as readers needs to be based on some understandings of 'reading' as an activity, and the previous section of this chapter presents a set of understandings that provide the intellectual and pedagogic framework for what follows. What comes next, therefore, is a development of some of the key aspects outlined above:

- The first, key understanding is that reading is an active process of making meaning(s), rather than a process of passive absorption. Simply reading a book does not guarantee that the facts, or the message, or the emotions contained in it will be 'transmitted' to the reader.

- Closely following the above point is the view, articulated in the first version of English in the National Curriculum, sometimes known as the Cox Report, that 'Reading is much more than the decoding of black marks upon a page: it is quest for meaning and one which requires the reader to be an active participant' (DES, 1989: para. 16.2).

- Reading engages a number of aspects of our humanity, to include an emotional dimension, imaginative engagement and involvement, and cognitive aspects (as we acquire information, for example).

- We bring ourselves to the texts we read: our culture, our gender, our social class, our history of life experiences. There is an interaction between what the writer offers in the text and what the reader brings to it from life. The consequence is that particularly literary texts, but not exclusively, are capable of having many meanings. As teachers, we need to develop pupils so that they can present an argued case, based on textual evidence, for the responses that spring from their understandings of the text in question, and how those responses are influenced by their own experiences of life and other texts.

- As teachers, we need to know about a range of reading skills, to include skimming and scanning, as well as the particular reading requirements of different kinds of texts.

- We also need to be knowledgeable about the development of reading competence (how pupils learn to read), and the developmental phases in reading development (see Dean, 2000; Millard, 1994).

■ Allied to the above point is the aim of enabling pupils to 'read against the text', either as a way of avoiding the tyranny of dominant interpretations, or as a way of exploring the possibilities for a range of meanings in a text.

WHAT ARE THE PEDAGOGIC IMPLICATIONS?

In the next part of this section there follow some indications of ways to develop pupils as readers by using literary texts. But first, it is important to note the emphasis on 'develop pupils as readers', and reinforce some points made earlier in this chapter. As secondary teachers we are still teaching pupils to read, not in the sense of developing the decoding and meaning-making skills that are properly the domain of our primary colleagues, but in the sense of continuing to develop their skills as they progress towards greater independence in their ability to read critically and reflectively.

1. The work of Lunzer and Gardner (1979) is rightly still very influential – despite its age. They developed a set of activities called DARTS – Directed Activities Related to Texts. The activities are designed:

(a) to encourage active approaches to texts

(b) to use problem-solving techniques

(c) to foster group and pair work with texts, involving collaborative talk

(d) to encourage an approach where multiple meanings are possible and valuable

(e) to demystify the notion of 'text'

(f) to enable pupils to communicate their findings in a variety of ways, to themselves and others.

To illustrate the approach:

• A teacher wants to develop pupils' understanding of narrative sequence and the linguistic cues that are so important. A short story is cut up into paragraphs, jumbled up, and placed in an envelope. Pupils are asked, in small groups, to recreate the story, and to prepare reasons why they have ordered the story in that way. This activity involves a degree of kinaesthetic learning as the pupils try to solve 'the problem'.

- To focus pupils on the choices made by a poet at word-level, a teacher prepares a copy of a poem with all the colour words deleted. Pupils are asked to fill in the gaps with colour words of their choosing. The pupils' versions of the poem are placed alongside the original, and rationales for the pupils' and the poet's choices are explored.

- DARTS activities can include role play, 'hot seating' and other classroom drama activities. For example, pupils studying Shakespeare's *Romeo and Juliet* are preparing a tribunal. Some pupils are preparing to be the parents of Romeo and Juliet. They will appear at the tribunal to answer questions about their roles in the deaths of the two young people. Other pupils are preparing the questions they want to ask. Meanwhile, other pupils are preparing to be members of the tribunal, and researching the questions they intend to put to the parents of Romeo and Juliet. When the preparation is finished, the tribunal is convened, with the teacher (or a pupil) acting as chairperson. (The same approach could culminate in an Oprah Winfrey type television show, a format more familiar to most pupils.)

These activities are a long way from the traditional ways of responding to literary texts, that is, the literary critical essay. Nevertheless, DARTS approaches may act very well as preliminary explorations of texts before moving to a more scholarly and academic presentation of the evidence for an interpretation.

2. The teaching of poetry has been singled out for particular emphasis, and there is a prevalent view that poetry is not well taught. DARTS activities provide a way of making poetry more accessible, and supporting pupils in moving away from a view of poetry that sees poems as having one correct but hidden meaning that needs to be extracted. In addition, it is important to emphasize how poems can engage a set of emotional responses, and that we very often ought to respond to poems with our hearts rather than with our intellects. That raises a whole set of issues about the development of a vocabulary to empower all pupils to be able so to respond. In addition, there is a

more general case for acknowledging the affective domain in so many aspects of life and literature, and for encouraging the articulation of emotional responses as legitimate ways of communicating reactions and responses. (For further more general reading on that topic, please consult the work of Goleman [1996].)

3. Throughout this book, range is an important word. Pupils have an entitlement to benefit from the English/Literacy teacher's expertise in the variety of texts to be accessed. In terms of literary texts, it is a problem knowing where to begin and where to end. As well as celebrating and enjoying the range, we also need to give due emphasis to the fact that different texts often require us to read them in different ways. Thus there are possibilities for specific interventions in pupils' experiences of texts, by indicating to and exploring with pupils the skills and techniques required. So we teach specific skills for specified purposes. At a possibly later stage, it is possible to develop in pupils the skills to investigate for themselves the ways that texts require them to read. How we cope with graphical novels, for example, seems to be highly complex, and yet even some reluctant readers will choose to read a comic where many of the graphical novel reading skills are required. Devising an investigative approach to developing reading competence is an aspect of current practice that is underused and ripe for development.

4. Whenever reading is mentioned in this book, there have been references to textual transformations. Any activity that results in pupils rereading a text for a purpose will be valuable; rereading is hard to encourage, given that for most readers 'getting through the book' is the prime aim of reading. However, there is merit in rereading, in that it provides chances to explore how texts manipulate the reader, how expectations and anticipations are created, and a whole range of aspects of the writer's craft, including scene setting and character creation. But asking them to pause, or reread, or start again is seen as an obstacle to the main activity, i.e., finishing the book. However, asking pupils to use one text to make another can be a way of giving purpose to rereading and enabling a problem-solving approach to be

used so that pupils can show knowledge and understanding. Some brief examples may help:

(a) Some A level students studying Thomas Hardy's *Tess of the D'Urbervilles* were asked to present ideas for an opera based on the novel. The students were asked to make a careful selection of key scenes, with a rationale, in terms of the opera, for their choices.

(b) Some Year 10 Media Studies pupils were getting to grips with storyboards as part of the process of creating a moving image text. They were also studying a play script version of *Billy Liar*, based on the novel by Keith Waterhouse, for their GCSE English Literature course. Using the play script, the film of the novel and their insights into how storyboards work, the pupils considered the implications for a twenty-first century remake of the film of the novel resulting in a storyboard for a crucial scene in the film.

(c) A Year 7 class is following a unit of study on a collection of poems about animals. The sequence of lessons culminates in pupils writing a poem that could be added to the small anthology they have been using. The teacher then introduces the pupils to some commercially produced poem posters. The posters are explored as texts, and the notion of 'recipe' is introduced (what elements in what proportions go together to make a poem poster?). The pupils design and produce a poem poster for a poem of their choosing from the anthology, and do the same thing with their own poem.

LITERATURE IN THE ENGLISH/LITERACY CURRICULUM

■ A BRIEF HISTORY TO LOCATE LITERATURE IN THE CURRICULUM

For many people, English equals Literature. The majority of graduates entering teacher training for secondary English come from a Literature degree background – perhaps you yourself are one such person. There is nothing wrong in that, of course, and in many ways the study of Literature prepares students very well for becoming a teacher of English in secondary schools.

However, as this book makes clear, English in schools and colleges is a many-faceted subject, comprising aspects of what in universities are seen as separate and distinct disciplines: Literature, Linguistics, Media and Drama, to name but four.

At the same time, we need to acknowledge that for many years the study of literature and the resourcing of English lessons with predominantly literary material dominated the English educational agenda and pupils' textual diet.

Some brief historical background is important here, because the debates about the nature of English as a school subject still reverberate with the intellectual and political clashes of the past. This book by its very nature is part of that ongoing debate and discussion, in the sense that it contributes to a set of understandings that inform our current awareness of what works best for learners in the field of literacy. (For a fuller insight into the cross currents of debate about the nature of English as an academic subject, you would do well to consult such writers as Belsey [1988] and Eagleton [1996].)

While those debates are interesting and important, we are more concerned here with the implications for what happens in secondary classrooms. First, a little history is necessary to give the current ideologies and practices some context.

The Cox Report (DES, 1989), the first version of English in the National Curriculum, describes five models of English (paragraphs 2.20–2.27), in an attempt to describe a set of views about English in secondary schools. Three of those models are of direct relevance to this historical background:

- personal growth
- cultural heritage
- cultural analysis.

A personal growth view of English emphasizes the importance of:

> literature in developing children's imaginative and aesthetic lives.
>
> **(Ibid.: para. 2.21)**

A cultural heritage model:

> emphasise[s] the responsibility of schools to lead children to an appreciation of those works of literature that have been widely regarded as amongst the finest in the language.
>
> **(Ibid.: para. 2.24)**

Notice how literature is privileged in both those definitions – it is through literature that we develop aesthetically and imaginatively, and access crucial features of a cultural (notice: not just literary) heritage.

When we get to the definition of a cultural analysis view of English, we notice some important differences. This view emphasizes:

> the role of English in helping children towards a critical understanding of the world and cultural environment in which they live. Children should know about the processes by which meanings are conveyed, and about the ways in which print and other media carry values.
>
> **(Ibid.: para. 2.25)**

Notice how 'literature' has been replaced by 'print and other media', a much broader definition embracing a much wider set of texts. There are other important distinctions to be teased out of the definition, and you may want to ponder the new emphases on 'processes', 'world and cultural environment' and 'critical understanding'.

However, central to the argument here is that there is a view of English that is counter to the hegemony of literary study and appreciation. But that tradition is a great and strong one. Until the middle of the twentieth century, literary study as an academic discipline was dominated by debates about:

■ 'good taste'

■ who and what are the greats of English Literature

■ what should students (at A level, at university) be studying in literature.

That is a slight caricature, but the substantive point here is crucial: literature was predominantly seen as the means by which 'civilizing values' were communicated and preserved for future generations. Students educated in and persuaded by that tradition became teachers of English, thus ensuring the preservation of the dominance of the 'personal growth' and 'cultural heritage' views of the subject.

The challenge came from those who would now put themselves into the 'cultural analysis' camp, that is, those who saw texts – of whatever kind – as culturally determined both in the ways they are created and how they are consumed. Not only does that allow for a broader definition of what constitutes a text, it also validates:

■ the consideration of how texts are constructed (processes)

■ by whom (institutions)

■ who they are made for (audiences)

■ how they make selections and representations of individuals and groups (representation)

■ how different media can create different kinds of texts (genre).

Already the thinking has moved a million miles away from 'the finest' and 'heritage'.

The teaching of English has also been influenced by movements in literary critical theory, and there are many points of connection between pedagogic developments and literary critical theory. The reader is directed to the work of Benton and Fox (1985), Burton (1989), Hunt (1991) and Peim (1993) for further details about a range of literary critical perspectives and their applicability to the secondary classroom. Some have been more beneficial than others, but current views of English, as presented via the Key Stage 3 Framework and recent developments at A level, are evidently influenced by changes in the world of literary critical theory.

That is a massive exercise in condensing the work of generations, so it is necessary for you to dip into the writing on this topic, as recommended above. But a worked example may help, especially when beginning to consider the implications for the classroom.

At one time, literary critics debated the relative merits of conflicting interpretations of any one text. In the case of *Hamlet*, for example, is it:

- Shakespeare tangling with notions of 'tragedy' (genre theory)?
- an Elizabethan critique of the uses and abuses of power (the text in its historical context)?
- Shakespeare as Hamlet (biographical studies)?
- Hamlet psychoanalysed (Freudian interpretation)?
- a study of some of the great civilizing issues of any age (thematic study for personal growth)?
- a study of personal endeavour v. state power (Marxist interpretation)?
- an example of English Literature at its finest (literary heritage view)?
- an insecure text (there are three versions), ascribed somewhat insecurely to Shakespeare (bibliographical/editorial approach)?

In recent times, instead of implying that a choice has to be made among competing interpretations, the view is very much that, so long as the argument is secure, there is the possibility of many interpretations of the same text. To go further, there is an inevitability about a polysemic view when one considers that the text will inevitably mean different things to people in different ages encountering the text in different cultures and contexts. We have only to recall the experience of rereading, say, a novel after a gap of some years. It is not the same book! And that is because the reader is not the same person, and the context of the reading is likely to be different.

Such a view, then, validates a range of possible interpretations. In the world of literary critical theory, we should turn to Reader-Response Theory for a fuller explanation of that view of how readers make meanings from texts (an accessible explanation of central aspects of reader-response theory is to be found in Chapter 1 of Dias and Hayhoe [1988]). In brief, such a view recognizes the importance of what the reader brings to the text, in terms of culture, race, gender, social class, age, experience of life and the like. The meaning-making process is about the interaction of text and reader, as opposed to the view that the text contains a meaning inserted by the writer for the reader to extract.

If this is the first time you have considered such views, then you are probably feeling a bit shell-shocked. If, on the other hand, you have been nodding in agreement, then you must be feeling relieved. Whatever your thoughts at this moment, it is time to pause to consider the implications of this challenge to literature and a particular view of its educative role.

What follows are some questions to prompt your thinking about the above. Give yourself time to consider them, jot down some thoughts, and allow yourself to respond to the views expressed above:

- In what ways could the study of soap opera be justified educationally?
- How could you make the study of, say, Hamlet fit the cultural analysis approach?
- What are the implications for 'culture' and 'heritage' in the multicultural and multilingual classroom?

▓ DISTINCTIVE FEATURES OF LITERATURE

One of the things this book emphasizes is the notion of 'text'. The excitement of teaching English/Literacy in large part resides in the variety of texts we can use to resource pupils' learning for a variety of purposes. Good English teachers constantly ask themselves: 'Which texts shall I select to enable my pupils to learn (about) x?'

For many of us, that question develops from our own engagement with texts; we tend to be collectors of all sorts of texts that we can use in the classroom, so we often start by saying: 'That's an interesting text; I could use that to teach y.'

Whatever way round we operate best, it comes down to the fundamental point: if we know about a rich variety of texts, and we know how to plan and prepare for pupils' learning, we can bring those two elements – textual knowledge and pedagogic understanding – together in our lessons and units of study.

What follows is a set of statements that develop the argument presented above. While being separate and distinctive statements, they interlock, supporting and developing a holistic view of the subject:

1. Most English teachers are most familiar with literary texts (given the academic background of the vast majority of English teachers), and there is merit in making pedagogic use of the rich variety of texts that come under the heading of literature.

2. There is, therefore, an important genre consideration when planning for the range of texts pupils encounter in classrooms.

3. Literary texts also enable us to explore some of the distinctive features of literary language; in other words, we need to define the distinctiveness of literary texts in part through their special uses of language.

4. It is fairly easy to generate lists of poetic and literary devices, and there is some merit in enabling pupils to seek them out and correctly identify them. However, to avoid the 'spot a simile' syndrome, we need to enable pupils to see that writers make linguistic choices for particular effects, so that the choice of, say, simile, is at the same time not to choose metaphor.

5. There is much value in tackling literary texts from a linguistic perspective, the so-called stylistic approach. Using the National Literacy Strategy's categories of word-, sentence- and text-level study, there is much to be derived from seeing the choices that writers make:

(a)   What other word(s) could the writer have chosen instead of … ?

(b)   Why did the writer choose compound sentences when there could have been a string of simple sentences? Rewrite it that way, and examine the differences.

(c)   What is so special about choosing a poem for that

moment? What is gained/lost by turning it into a
newspaper article?

Such approaches focus on the 'constructedness' of texts, that texts are the
outcome of choices. The Cox Report (DES, 1989) reminds us that the word
'poet' comes from the Greek 'to make'. Poets are makers, and in a memorable turn of phrase, the document goes on to say that 'reading is a quest
for meaning' (DES, 1989: para. 16.2). The authors remind us that reading
is a process of making meanings from the texts of others, while writing is
about making meanings in one's own texts – throughout there is the
emphasis on 'making meanings', in a variety of ways.

All of that theoretically supported viewpoint connects strongly with
pedagogic understandings that inform good practice in English/Literacy
teaching:

- It is recognized as good practice to acknowledge and value
  what pupils bring to the lesson, in terms of language,
  existing understandings (sometimes mistaken, but they are
  a starting point), cultural insights and experiences.

- The ways of investigating texts advocated above encourage
  an active approach to classroom tasks.

- The process of writing in particular is demystified by
  taking the approach that emphasizes authorial choices –
  the approach works both for the pupils' own writing
  development as well as their engagement with the writings
  of others.

- Making meanings from particularly literary texts is not
  about getting 'the right answer', but presenting a well
  supported argument for a view, drawing on a range of
  evidence from the text.

- There are a variety of ways of communicating
  understanding of a literary text – the literary critical essay
  need not predominate.

- Of particular interest might be:
  - imaginative responses to literary texts ('Lady Macbeth's
    Diary')
  - textual transformations (the newspaper reports of
    Macbeth's demise)
  - textual migrations (the storyboard of the opening scene

> of *Macbeth;* redesigning the cover of the printed version of the play)
>
> – a performed modern version
>
> – preparing questions for the imagined interrogation of Macbeth.

The hope here is that, as well as getting some interesting possible classroom activities, you can also see the connections to theoretical perspectives. We want our pupils to:

- engage in active learning
- have 'ownership' of meanings and interpretations, within a rigorous framework for their learning
- learn with others, to check their meanings (from their own texts, from the texts of others) against each other
- develop their own perspectives, and have the skills to argue and present them
- see texts as accessible on their terms, for reading and writing purposes
- enjoy reading and writing texts
- make deliberate and justifiable choices for reading and writing purposes through reflection ('What reading skills do I need to make sense of this text?' 'What is the best choice of text to create so as to get my meaning across?').

The above examples illustrate the combining of theory from another discipline, i.e., literary criticism, with pedagogy, bringing both together for effective learning opportunities.

It would be dishonest to imply that the issue of canonical texts and their place in the school curriculum has gone away or been completely replaced by other understandings. The National Curriculum names Shakespeare as the only writer who has to be studied; in addition, pupils have to be assessed on their knowledge of Shakespeare, however that is defined. Furthermore, there is the requirement to study literary texts from before and after 1914, with supplied suggestions for writers. Whenever lists are provided in such contexts, issues of the canon still exist.

However, there has been enough debate over recent years to lay to rest the idea that there are absolute comparative values to be ascribed to selected texts. From the other side of the argument, the idea that all texts are simply texts is equally problematic (however attractive such a reductive view might seem as a way of avoiding the vexed question of 'value'). Therefore, there have to be other ways of making appropriate value judgements about texts.

There seem to be two viable ways forward:

1. Gunther Kress (1995) helpfully describes certain texts as 'culturally privileged', thus leaving the way open for an exploration with pupils of 'culture' and 'privilege': whose culture, who decides? Certain texts are central to culture, but the notion of culture shifts depending on who you are. Pupils need to know that they can privilege texts by their actions, of buying and reading, of going to films, of watching television programmes.

2. There is merit in having a pedagogic rationale for the choice of a text: 'this text has been chosen because it illustrates the use of [defined feature]'. The strength of such an argument lies in the learning potential of the text within the parameters of the National Curriculum, the Key Stage 3 Framework, and the GCSE and A level syllabuses. Issue of cultural worth and universal import are subsumed by a set of professional and educational imperatives – in that sense, the teacher's subject knowledge becomes professional knowledge in a very powerful way.

▒ INTERIM THOUGHTS

The status of literature, the role of literature, the purpose of literature, the centrality of literature: all those topics have been the subjects of debates and disagreements since books first started to appear. And there is no sign that the discussion is going to come to an end.

Literature in education is additionally a politically sensitive topic, connecting as it does in some influential people's minds with aspects of culture, heritage and national identity. Threaten to move the assessment of Shakespeare from English to English Literature, for example, and there are immediate and powerful protests – 'How can you study English without Shakespeare?' some people assert.

But in an increasingly multicultural and multilingual society, in schools where pupils come from a variety of social classes and educational backgrounds, and where teachers come to the teaching of English from backgrounds in Linguistics, Media Studies, Cultural Studies, as well as Literature (see Chapter 1 for the variety of ways 'Literature' can be defined and studied), it is no wonder that the notion of English as a school subject is richly problematic. But in that richness is the excitement, for the domain of literature provides so much that is educationally valuable. The next part of the chapter will explore in more detail some of the ways literature can provide distinctive learning opportunities within the statutory and advisory frameworks for English and Literacy.

But first, a pause moment.

PAUSE

What follows is a sample Unit of Study on a literary text. The aim of the example is to:

- demonstrate how literature can provide distinctive learning opportunities
- provide a sample template for planning a Unit of Study.

Task No. 1:

Read the Unit carefully, and make clear to yourself how it implements some of the principles referred to above.

A Sample Unit of Study: Based on a Literary Text

Preamble

This is an example of a 'mini-unit of study', that is, one that lasts less time than the norm. Most Units of Study in secondary schools/colleges are designed to last about half a term. For the sake of accessibility, this is deliberately shorter.

In this instance, the Unit is intended to last for twelve lessons over four weeks, with a Year 8 mixed-ability class of boys and girls. Each lesson lasts one hour. The particular focus of this Unit is some aspects of Science Fiction writing, with a particular focus on *The End of the World* by Arthur C. Clarke.

You have:

- a sheet defining learning objectives – with gaps for you to map the objectives onto the National Curriculum and the Framework
- an 'at-a-glance' plan of the Unit (Figure 5.1)
- a suggested plan for the opening lesson.

UNIT PLAN
LEARNING OBJECTIVES: CURRICULUM COVERAGE
Year 8
Science Fiction/Arthur C. Clarke

Indicate clearly how you have drawn from relevant English documentation:
Framework for KS3, NC 2000, GCSE or AL syllabus objectives etc.
[Code for Framework reference: W1 = Word Level Objective, Sn1 = Sentence-Level Objective. Ensure that one Key Objective is included in each unit plan.
Indicate in bold.]

Ref. to Framework for English, NC2000, GCSE or AL objectives	Learning Objectives
[TASK for Reader: Please supply the necessary references!]	**Speaking and Listening** • Be able to talk about and discuss aspects of the story/genre for specific purposes and audiences • Be able to use process talk appropriately **Reading** • Know about specified narrative devices associated with this genre • Know the associated terminology (narrative sequence, suspense, genre, narrator) • Be able to access other science fiction texts **Writing** • Be able to write in the science fiction style • Show understanding of narrative 'gaps' by using them in their writing

	WEEK 1	WEEK 2	WEEK 3	WEEK 4	Evolving/changing ideas
Content	• Narrative devices in Science Fiction	• Developing narrative features, to include Interior Monologue	• Performing Interior Monologue • Read additional SciFi text from library	• Writing, Reading, S & L	
Teaching and Learning Activities		• Working on missing moments • Working with 'response partner' • Writing interior monologue	• Preparing, rehearsing, performing • Giving positive feedback • Reading	• Finish SciFi text • Write opening of sequel to the story • Take part in group presentation • Review Unit	
Resources		• Extracts from story	• Library resources prepared in advance – liaise with Librarian	• Library resources • Task sheet for presentation	
	• *The End of the World*, Arthur C. Clarke				

FIGURE 5.1 AT-A-GLANCE UNIT PLAN

ENGLISH LESSON PLAN   **DATE:**
TOPIC: Lesson 1: Science Fiction Unit of Study
YEAR/ABILITY GROUP: 8 (mixed ability)   **DURATION**: 60 mins

LEARNING OBJECTIVES *(refer to objectives in unit plan)*
All pupils should:
Know about Science Fiction
Understand main features of the genre
Be able to identify some genre features from the story

ATs: En1 – 1f
En2 – 1h, 1j, 8c
More able pupils should:
Be able to identify a greater range of genre features
Be able to provide a rationale for authorial choices

TEACHING AND LEARNING ACTIVITIES

Teaching Activity	Learning Activity	Approx. Time
Entry, settle, register	Listening	5 mins
Whole-class phase: introduction of new story, learning aims shared, displayed		5 mins
Teacher leads whole class mindmap on SciFi	Contributions	10 mins
Teacher draws out main genre features	Note taking	10 mins
Teacher reading opening page to class		5 mins
Describe group activity	Groups to: Find genre features Suggest additions to genre list Prepare for feedback	10 mins
Organize feedback, points on board	Group contributions	10 mins
Trailer for next lesson	Tidy away, wait for dismissal	5 mins

DIFFERENTIATED SUPPORT *(e.g. your plans for SEN, EAL etc.)*:
Mainly relying on differentiation of outcome: modelling at outset to help less confident. Teacher to select groups to ensure balance of ability

ICT USE:

ASSESSMENT OPPORTUNITY:

Group work will allow targeted teacher assessment of Speaking and Listening e.g. 'Contribute to and respond constructively in discussion, advocating and justifying a point of view'

HOMEWORK:

N/A

RESOURCES:

Story, paper and pens, books for note taking

FOR NEXT TIME:

Task No. 2:

Now it is over to you!

1. Choose a literary text, and create your own Unit of Study, using the example above as a template.

2. How could the layout of the Unit be more 'user friendly', i.e., by using ICT? Have a go at creating your document with a word processor, or desktop publisher or presentation software.

3. You could then plan the opening lesson, using the schema above. Please feel free to adapt the layout – the important thing is to experiment so as to find what works for you, at the same time as you fulfil the requirements for effective planning. Above all else, you need to show that you understand the principles behind planning.

4. The Unit and the individual lesson have been created with the National Curriculum for English very much in mind. It would be an interesting activity to map the Unit and the lesson onto the Framework, to see what would remain and what would have to change to meet a somewhat distinctive and separate set of requirements.

5. If you were to use the above resource with a Year 10 or 11 class, doing GCSE, what changes would you make, bearing in mind the requirements of the syllabuses for English and English Literature?

OPPORTUNITIES FOR DISTINCTIVE LEARNING

Detailed consideration has already been given earlier in this chapter to reading in general terms and with particular reference to the study of literature. We now need to give some thought to those other ATs in English: Speaking and Listening, and Writing.

▓ LITERATURE AND SPEAKING AND LISTENING

Literature provides us with a rich variety of texts specifically designed for performance or to be spoken aloud. At whole-text level, it is possible to explore and examine the special features of texts – linguistically, structurally – that indicate that they are for some kind of performance. Starting with play scripts, this approach could develop into explorations of film/television scripts, and radio scripts.

From that beginning, it is possible to see a clear rationale for pupils creating their own scripts, using the provided examples as models, and employing the distinctive features discovered and described:

- At whole-text level, there is the possibility of pupils identifying the textual features they have employed, in their own writing, or in the work of other pupils.

- For Speaking and Listening assessment criteria, performances of scripts (their own or written by others) could be evaluated against a set of criteria negotiated with the pupils and derived from the National Curriculum Programme of Study.

Poetry has been identified as a problematic area of the English curriculum; poetry seems to present a set of special challenges to both teachers and pupils. One way to make poetry more accessible is through performance, by listening to poems being read aloud by poets and performers, and by pupils preparing and presenting their own performances of poems, solo or in groups. Dramatic renditions of some poems can really bring them to life and can enhance understanding.

In general terms, it is always wise to present pupils with an example or a model, first to explore, and then to imitate or even emulate. Listening to poets reading their own works can provide wonderful insights, whether it is John Hegley in the present or Robert Frost in the past. Ideally, a live performance by a poet can have a memorable effect on pupils.

The next stage is to define potential audiences for a poetry performance, live or recorded. Then, a set of 'success criteria' can be defined, for the listening phase of the project. In that way, a whole set of viable Speaking and Listening aspects are addressed:

- aspects of 'process talk', as decisions are made (most likely in groups), rehearsals managed and evaluated, final performances prepared

- aspects of 'talk in the group', as people give feedback, manage the dynamic and move things forward

- aspects of 'performance', evaluated and/or assessed against criteria.

There exist some anthologies where poems to be read aloud have been collected; Beasley (1994) and Kitchen (1988) are good starting places.

Moving away from poetry, interesting though it is as a special case in this context, there are many opportunities with literary texts to address both major aspects of Speaking and Listening, that is, process talk and performance talk. Most of the following suggestions are in some ways developments of points already made, but put those aspects in a more general literary context:

- Audio books are popular and readily available, providing models for pupils' own examples.

- Transforming 'print texts' into texts that rely on spoken words – book into play, play into film, book into radio play/'Book at Bedtime' serialization.

Whatever is attempted, there is much to recommend a Speaking and Listening approach to literary texts. We need to move our pupils away from seeing literature as some kind of crossword puzzle to be 'solved', and more towards an approach which enables a range of meanings to be presented, debated and rationalized. Speaking and Listening activities open up the range of possibilities.

LITERATURE AND WRITING

Elsewhere in the book, writing has been considered in depth. Therefore, there is no need to repeat principles and practices already covered. Nevertheless, there is value in establishing here some distinctive perspectives on writing in the context of the study of literary texts.

A straightforward distinction when we consider literature and writing is:

- writing about literary texts

- writing literary texts.

There is no great profundity in that; however, it is important to see what for some is the dominant mode of writing about literature, the so-called 'literary critical essay', in a broader context. Writing about literary texts is an important skill, and needs to be done in a variety of ways. Even in the respectable world of literary criticism, there is a variety of text types, in addition to the literary critical essay:

- reviews
- commentaries
- annotations
- letters to the editor
- replies and rejoinders
- parodies and pastiches.

CONCLUSION

Our aim as teachers of English is to enable our pupils to articulate their responses and reactions to, and their understanding of, all sorts of texts – a principle that follows logically from the articulation of this book's over-arching approach to English and Literacy. In the end, we want our pupils to be able to implement the 'fitness for purpose' principle: 'To communicate what I want to say to this audience means that I have a choice to make from the available text types, and my judgement is that in this context the best way of communicating is via … '

In the process of leading pupils to that point, teachers introduce pupils to as wide a range of texts as possible, and enable them to use those texts for appropriate purposes in their own writing. We, therefore, ought to encourage a range of ways of responding to literary texts, to include the literary critical essay, but also to include many other ways of responding.

In addition, we ought not to ignore the importance of pupils writing their own literary texts. There is a view, still surviving but much challenged by recent developments in the research about and pedagogy of literacy, that sees English as the part of the curriculum where pupils learn to develop their creativity, their imaginations, and their ability to empathize, through the reading and writing of complete literary texts. (For an example, please see the letter in the *Times Educational Supplement* of 21 February 2003, entitled 'Authors unite against tests', for an articulation of that perspective. It is also worth noting that Melvin Burgess, Carol Ann Duffy, Philip Pullman and Michael Rosen – all well-known names in the sphere of children's literature – are among the signatories.)

In some ways, a false dichotomy is being created – it is unnecessarily limiting to see the matter as 'creativity' versus 'analysis', or 'whole books' versus 'extracts', or 'empathy' versus 'comprehension questions'. Learners need *all* those approaches to enable them to develop as confidently and competently literate people, and teachers need the skills to mix and match the techniques as appropriate to the learning needs of individuals and groups.

There is, therefore, a place for pupils to develop as writers of literary texts – but not exclusively. Literature is a peculiarly powerful medium, and it would be foolish to deny its impact. However, an approach that proclaims a hierarchical notion of texts – with literature at the summit – is less than helpful at a time when all of us are inundated with text types in profusion. Additionally, we ought never to lose sight of the informing principle – that we want our learners to be able to use as wide a range of text types as possible for their own communications, and we want literary texts to be among the options.

Throughout this chapter, the emphasis has been on developing pupils as readers, so that they become critical, engaged and reflective. In addition, pupils need to be able to articulate their responses in a variety of ways, using creative and imaginative responses as well as more analytical techniques. Literary texts provide ample opportunities and examples to resource those learning aims. We need to see ourselves as teachers of reading (who use literary texts among many others to resource pupils' learning opportunities) rather than teachers of literature. In that way, we avoid the convolutions of the cultural heritage debate, and instead focus on the learning aims of the National Curriculum (Speaking and Listening, Reading, Writing) and the National Literacy Strategy (word-, sentence-, text-level study), using our textual knowledge and expertise to make informed pedagogic decisions about texts to study and to provide exemplars. In that sense we are on firm ground – we are making decisions that impact on our teaching and pupils' learning, rather than providing a cultural rationale, in terms of communicating a heritage, that increasingly appears problematic and unsustainable.

KEY TEXTS

Benton, M. and Fox, G. (1985) *Teaching Literature 9 to 14*. Oxford: Oxford University Press.

Dean, G. (2000) *Teaching Reading in Secondary Schools*. London: David Fulton.

Hunt, P. (1991) *Criticism, Theory, and Children's Literature*. Oxford: Blackwell.

CHAPTER SIX

Oracy in English

KEY FEATURES OF THE AREA OF STUDY

■ THE HISTORICAL CONTEXT

It is worth reviewing the separation of Speaking and Listening into a distinct Attainment Target in the first version of the National Curriculum (DES, 1989), in that its inclusion was a significant step in validating 'oracy', a term deliberately coined as equivalent to literacy and hence to include not only the range and variety of spoken discourses we engage in but also the importance of having confident command of this range of language choices. Originally formulated by Professor Andrew Wilkinson, the term 'oracy' was introduced to describe 'adequacy in speaking and adequacy in listening' (1965: 177), in a series of articles about the importance of explicit speaking and listening activities, using real spoken material, taped in classrooms and analysed according to linguistic principles.

In one of the articles, Wilkinson's rationale for oracy in the classroom strikes a particularly topical note, which could be directly transferred to the Citizenship curriculum in 2003;

> To give the pupil … a productive linguistic role implies a different relationship with the teacher, which many teachers find hard to accept. To give the pupil as potential citizen such a role is to encourage social change to produce freer citizens.
>
> (Wilkinson, 1968: 13)

Carter reminds us that oracy refers to 'the development of the skills of speaking and listening', which 'develops the skills of reading and writing' (1995: 113). There is nevertheless a significant difference between the two areas in that reading and writing have to be explicitly taught, whereas speaking and listening are initially acquired naturally.

By placing the responsibility on English teachers to use the primary means of human communication as a method of learning and a way of developing language use, the NC nevertheless made a powerful statement about the centrality of spoken language and its relationship to learning. It incidentally also made a powerful implicit statement about inclusion. Since talk is a naturally social phenomenon, contexts which exploit the value of talking as an aid to learning can be constructed to ensure participation by all pupils.

In 1987, the National Oracy Project (NOP) was established in order to emphasize and develop the role of spoken language in both teaching and learning in all curriculum areas. Norman (1992) describes the work of the project from its inception through to its dissemination phase (1987–93), which spanned the introduction of the National Curriculum.

The Project's aims (ibid.: xii) were:

- to enhance the role of speech in the learning process 5–16 by encouraging active learning
- to develop the teaching of oral communication skills
- to develop methods of assessment of and through speech, including assessment for public examinations at 16+
- to improve pupils' performance across the curriculum
- to enhance teachers' skills and practice
- to promote recognition of the value of oral work in schools and increase its use as a means of improving learning.

Most children begin school with well-developed speaking abilities; the planned and purposeful development of all forms of oracy provides a natural starting point for encouraging learning. Beyond that, it can also help them learn social codes which they do not inherently recognize or use. As Neelands points out: 'Many young people encounter difficulties in their social lives precisely because they haven't accessed or recognised the need to respond to and manage the prevailing codes and conventions ... ' (1992: 20).

■ CURRENT CONCERNS

The 'prevailing codes and conventions' referred to above presumably take the form of standard English (SE). A definition of SE is provided in Chapter 2. It is arguable whether *telling* a pupil to use spoken standard English (DfEE, 1999) will ensure understanding of that form, whereas providing a context in which pupils recognize that spoken SE would be used (e.g., in news programmes) creates an opportunity to add SE to their repertoire. Moreover, it allows the device of an adopted role at once to distance and thus to protect the speaker's own cultural, social or linguistic identity.

The desirable aim of adding SE to a speaker's repertoire is simple to state but not quite so unproblematic to achieve. For a start, definitions of SE are slippery because:

- they need to be qualified by the recognition that SE is subject to change across its spoken and written forms (e.g., the grammar of spoken SE is not the same as for written SE because each variety is governed by different rules and conventions)

- the vocabulary and grammar of SE change over time (e.g., the meaning of 'disinterested' in a Jane Austen novel is 'impartial', whereas it has come to mean 'uninterested' to many contemporary speakers)

- the use of a grammatical construction such as 'we were all *sat* on the bus … ', where SE would expect *sitting*, is currently in the process of change

- SE changes according to the audience, purpose and context of its use (we speak differently when asking the bank manager for a loan from the way we speak in a relaxed social situation).

However, allowing for complexities of both form and function, a useful starting point for understanding SE in an educational context is the first version of the NC English (DES, 1989). Despite the emphasis on spoken SE in the current version of the NC English, it is worth returning to the legacy of the NOP to reaffirm the effectiveness of its principles and practices in the classroom. We need only to read the Introduction to the booklet from the KS3 National Strategy, *Year 7 Speaking and Listening Bank* (DfEE, 2001d) to revisit both the rationale and the strategies proposed by the NOP.

Your reading of Chapter 2, and this chapter up to this point, have presented a picture of the complex web of spoken language. Because it is such a complex topic, and because teachers need to be confident about their understanding of these issues, it may be worth pausing for a moment to summarize where this study has taken us as 'scholars of language'.

Summary of key points relating to spoken language and oracy:

- Pupils' skills in spoken language deserve as much attention as their skills in reading and writing.
- Spoken and written varieties of language differ but both belong to rule-governed systems of language formed by sound, grammar and meaning.
- Standard English is a social (as distinct from regional) dialect, the spoken variety of which can use any accent: dialect is the grammatical and lexical organization of a language; accent is the pronunciation features.
- SE is the prestige variety of English dialects but it is not a fixed entity – it changes over time and according to the audience, purpose and context of its use.
- As the most prestigious variety, SE wields most power, which leads to the frequent misunderstanding that it is 'correct' or 'proper' English – it is simply different.
- In classrooms, pupils need to be explicitly taught about what SE is, where it comes from and how it is used.
- Through active investigations of language use, the aim is to add SE to pupils' repertoires of spoken English, the variety they would select according to the context of its use.

ORACY DEVELOPED THROUGH CLASSROOM ACTIVITIES

The importance of providing 'real-life' audiences and purposes for the development of effective literacy is readily acknowledged. The publication, *Year 7 Speaking and Listening Bank* (DfEE, 2001d), for example, recognizes the need for a variety of 'real-life' contexts to enhance pupils' speaking and listening experiences. Its stated aim is to:

> Help pupils to sharpen their skills and develop confidence as speakers and listeners, by providing models, carefully planned activities and tasks that promote different kinds of talk and listening, and through structured reflection.
>
> (DfEE, 2001d: v)

By addressing nineteen Speaking and Listening objectives, as proposed by the KS3 Framework, the booklet offers valuable practical resources and teaching strategies, beside a coherent rationale which reminds us that speaking and listening are essential in defining literacy. Not only is spoken language the primary means of human communication, it is critical in developing and supporting writing skills from a very early age, as *Developing Early Writing* (DfEE, 2001e) reminds us.

In the classroom, 'real', active investigations of language in use can be devised from a wide range of familiar situations, from television quiz shows, to cookery demonstrations, courtroom drama to charity appeals, in order to present flexible opportunities which can be planned in a variety of ways, and which can explore all the Attainment Targets for English in appropriate depth. These 'real life' talk contexts in which the student operates in action as a live participant' (Neelands, 1992: 17) can be readily adapted to a range of ages and abilities according to the Learning Aims/Objectives specified. Most importantly,

> young people can try out audiences, registers and respond to purposes which are clearly defined and bound to the context. They can respond to the context and test out a wide range of points of view in a real way ...
>
> **(Neelands, 1992: 19)**

One particularly adaptable context-focused situation was originally devised by teachers and pupils engaged in the National Oracy Project. First encountered at an INSET session run by the pupils who had been taught it, it has since been adapted for use with initial teacher training (ITT) trainee teachers, who in turn have frequently adapted it during training placements and into their teaching appointments. The following description is capable of being adapted for use across age phases, lesson allocations and other constraints. It will depend very much on the objectives the teacher wishes to prioritize as to its length and development; it could last over an entire half term or be abbreviated as required.

THE URBANIA PROJECT

LEARNING AIMS/OBJECTIVES

These would depend on the precise focus which the teacher wishes to emphasize: decisions about whether to prioritize speaking, listening, group discussion and interaction, drama, standard English or language variation; what could be addressed at word, sentence and text levels (KS3 Framework) would be dependent on where this unit fitted in the particular department's units of study.

As preparation for the Urbania project, read 'The Role of Talk in Learning' by Douglas Barnes (1992).

■ PROCEDURE

It is important to stress that the following is not a plan; it provides an adaptable framework only and is described in the way we use it with trainee teachers:

- Mindmap 'Urbania' or wherever you choose to set the project.
- Explain the history of this small town with its church/castle/pub/school; highlight expanding tourist industry; establish some tensions caused by the development.
- Divide the class into small groups; allocate locations in the town to each group.
- Groups should include: castle, pub, school, church, gift shop. Other locations can be added as necessary.
- Groups draw or represent their location on a large sheet of sugar paper.
- Groups create characters who are attached to/live in that location.
- Character identities will be developed according to the amount of information and direction you as teacher provide.
- Develop identity of the town by each group 'presenting' their building, in character; teacher questions characters to draw out conflicts and tensions between traditionalists and developers.
- All contribute to map of town by grouping buildings around the square with its fountain (prepared in advance by teacher).
- Announce Town Council meeting; Urbania to become a theme park.
- Characters to speak for and against the proposal.
- Produce radio/television programmes for the protest/ support campaigns.

■ REFLECTION ON THE URBANIA PROJECT

> Some questions posed by the Urbania activity; make a note of your responses.
>
> How does mindmapping help establish the context?
>
> How does the teacher decide on the composition of the groups?
>
> How much information (including written descriptions) should the pupils be given about their location/characters?
>
> What should be the teacher's role throughout? Should she/he be participant or manager?

> Look at Speaking and Listening at KS3 and 4 in the NC; how many of the requirements are fulfilled by this activity? Consider the following areas of knowledge about language and how they could be planned for and evaluated in this project:
>
> • regional and social variation of accents and dialects
> • spoken standard English and when to use it
> • appropriate language choices related to context, purpose and audience
> • experience of a wide range of language for a variety of purposes and in a variety of roles
> • understanding the social, cultural and power relationships which determine how language is used.

ASSESSING ORACY

Perhaps it is timely to confront the view that oral language generally is difficult to assess. Audio and video recording devices constitute valid, reliable and informative evidence of achievement. If we are to acknowledge the real complexities and subtleties of assessment, it seems arguable that oracy should be at the forefront of curriculum assessment since an articulate command of spoken language, in a media and technology oriented society, is possibly the most important way of participating confidently in a democracy. Teachers therefore have responsibility for developing progression in pupils' oral abilities. Moreover, the process as well as the product of oral language needs to be assessed, which in turn raises questions about whether oral or social skills are being assessed. Standardizing tapes for GCSE English indicate that oral assessment cannot avoid recognition of social skills; nor, in my view, should it. By conceptualizing oral events as 'texts', as advocated by linguists, including Carter (1995), where social skills form part of the features within the linguistic framework, any contradictions automatically disappear.

The relationship between oracy, drama and pupils' social development has been amply supported by most of the sources referred to in this chapter. To avoid the challenge of assessment would be to deny the value and significance of this relationship.

In order to demonstrate how formative, summative, self and peer assessment may be built into a unit of work, the Urbania project could provide a starting point.

The following are suggestions representing opportunities for assessment. Final decisions about these would be closely related to the learning objectives for the unit:

- Formative: teacher observation of process; group skills, such as leading discussion, moving the debate on, contributing appropriately; language chosen for effective characterization.

- Peer: through evaluation sheets as pupils watch news presentations – criteria could include use of standard English/clarity and intonation/eye contact.

- Self: individual response to objectives for progress, set from formative observation/monitoring.

- Summative: presentation of a current affairs programme, debating the issues surrounding Urbania, teacher assessed and graded for KS3 or GCSE.

In order to demonstrate the relationship between the cycle of planning, teaching, managing, and assessing Speaking and Listening within English, we have chosen a recent example of a trainee teacher's work.

CASE STUDY: A TRAINEE TEACHER'S INVESTIGATION INTO AN ASPECT OF THE ENGLISH CURRICULUM, FOCUSING ON SPEAKING AND LISTENING WITH A YEAR 10 GROUP OF GIRLS

To explore an aspect of the English curriculum, a trainee English teacher, Kerry, chose to investigate the substantial difference in marks between written coursework and speaking and listening activities at Key Stage 4.

At her second placement school, where she taught from February to May 2002, she had been assigned a high-achieving Year 10 group, all girls, who were working on GCSE coursework. Kerry discovered that, although they were achieving consistently high marks for written work, their oral marks lagged significantly behind. For her investigation, she focused on three pupils who had the greatest discrepancy between written and oral marks. Her explicit aims for the assignment were:

- to bridge the gap between the Literature and the Speaking and Listening grade/mark

- to use drama and group work effectively in order to achieve this

- to ensure that talk is considered by staff and pupils to be a valuable and valid process as well as a product of learning.

The task, set prior to decisions about the topic for her assignment, was to teach the whole group a Wide Reading coursework unit (GCSE AQA syllabus). Kerry was given the opportunity to choose the texts, and to devise her own question within a unit of work which she designed. She chose the texts *Pride and Prejudice* by Jane Austen and *Ma Semblable Ma Soeur* by Michele Roberts for an essay comparing and contrasting the representation of women. She requires pupils to comment on 'the moral, social, historical and cultural implications of the texts; the writers' choice and use of language and form and their effects on the reader; the writers' narrative craft and appeal to the reader'.

The medium-term plan (Figure 6.1) also included 'as many objectives and opportunities for talk as was possible', which, in teaching it, resulted in the 'inclusion of talk in lessons varied, from using it as a means to achieving learning objectives in pairs, groups or in whole class discussion, to using talk as a way of displaying what they have learned in the lesson'. Kerry went on to describe and analyse the pupils' use of talk to 'gain an understanding of the texts' and her use of formative assessment 'to evaluate lessons and assess pupil learning'. (Note that assessment is incorporated into her medium-term plan.) Eventually the pupils arrived at the planning stage for their essay. Kerry engineered the task to be a collaborative one, so that in groups pupils planned their essays, within a framework which she had provided.

Pupils went on to write the first draft of their essay which was informally assessed in relation to the criteria in the title. The class was then set a Speaking and Listening task based on the process of preparing for their coursework assignment. The task was:

In groups of four or five, you are to use drama to explore a particular character from the texts we have studied. In your group, you are to devise a conversation, scene, situation involving the characters Lizzy, Rose, Lily and Lydia or Jane exploring women's role in society as seen by each character. You could consider the following: what women are/aren't allowed to do; education; family; a typical day in the life; job/career opportunities. This is an assessed piece and will be recorded using a video camera.

Although some of the pupils were reluctant to perform with their peers watching, Kerry was determined to record the lesson to have a permanent record of the performances, and to use it with a mentor to verify her judgements in an aspect of assessment where she was relatively inexperienced. In addition, she wanted the pupils to be able to see the product of their learning and hard work:

By allowing them to watch themselves at a later date, pupils will be able to see what they have achieved, to observe what their strengths are and … to set targets … where any improvements are needed … [to] … boost their confidence and self-evaluation skills.

Pupils were given the assessment criteria early in the process and each performance was praised and briefly evaluated with the audience also providing some peer evaluation, which was couched in positive, encouraging terms. Continuing the theme of assessment, Kerry continued:

When the performances were finished, I gave each pupil an evaluation sheet to fill in, in order to allow them to reflect on how well they believed they had worked towards and performed the assessed piece. [Pupils] identified their own starting points and set targets for future learning and achievement. This form of assessment is valuable as it gives pupils a degree of ownership in the assessment process, something that I wanted to maintain after the pupils had created and delivered their own performances …

The pupils were assessed on an individual basis according to GCSE criteria … [and] … each was discussed with the class teacher before settling on final marks.

The overall findings of the investigation were then considered;

Pupils B, V and W who were chosen as my sample made quite impressive progress. Their results were as follows:

- B achieved 45 marks (a comfortable grade A) for Literature and 38 marks for EN1 (a low grade B, a difference of 7 marks which is an improvement of 7 marks (almost an entire grade)
- V achieved 43 marks (a low grade A) for Literature and 45 marks for EN1 (a comfortable grade A), a difference of –2 marks which is an improvement of 10 marks. EN1 is now the highest mark
- W achieved 44 marks for Literature (a low grade A) and 45 marks for EN1 (a comfortable grade A), a difference of –1 mark, which is an improvement of 9 marks. As with pupil V, EN1 is now the highest mark.

Returning at this point to her original aims, to assess how far these have been met, Kerry provided evidence to show how the drama exercise improved the pupils' social and communication skills, as well as contributing to their improved GCSE scores. She also noted, from her observations and evaluations during teaching the unit, that 'the collaborative planning task and other group based activities involving talk, including the drama performance, were, ... a success and enabled the pupils to use each other as a resource for knowledge and gaining understanding'. Although careful not to make grandiose or sweeping claims, she concluded that she was developing 'strong beliefs about the potential of drama for enhancing pupil learning, not only in my own subject but also in other curriculum areas'. And the considerable improvement in the pupils' marks speaks for itself!

IN CONCLUSION

> In order to consolidate what you have learnt about spoken language and oracy, and to place it in a wider context of language, revisit the Audit of Language subject knowledge (Appendix 1), adding key points to summarize your learning.

KEY TEXTS

Norman, K. (ed.) (1992) *Thinking Voices: The Work of the National Oracy Project.* London: Hodder & Stoughton.

Sage, R. (2000) *Class Talk: Successful Learning through Effective Communication.* Stafford: Network Educational Press.

Question: Compare and contrast the presentation of women in Jane Austen's *Pride and Prejudice* and *Ma Semblable Ma Soeur* by Michele Roberts

	Week 1: 08/04/02	Week 2: 15/04/02	Week 3: 22/04/02	Week 4: 29/04/02	Week 5: 06/05/02
Content	Short story analysis	1) Feedback Michele Roberts research homework. Finish brainstorm notes about *Ma S Ma S* Feedback short story analysis 2) Construct comparison grid 3) Essay plan. Point, quote, comment	1) First draft of essay to be handed in. Video 2) Video 3) Feedback essay comments. Discuss any issues, problems	1) (P) To hand in final draft of essay. Begin discussion of S&L assessment 2) (P) to continue with S&L assessment. Practice time in groups 3) (P) to perform S&L assessments. To be recorded by video camera	2) Final lesson – (P) to finish S&L performances (T) to feedback essay marks/comments.
Teaching and Learning Activities	3) (P) to complete her short story question sheet focusing on *Ma S Ma S* Homework: to write a paragraph or two about the style of Roberts' short story and how it contributes to the presentation of women	1) (1) In pairs (P) to look over brainstorm notes from before holiday. 2) Feedback notes from other sections as a whole class on whiteboard. (3) Feedback short story analysis questions and discuss findings. Homework: (P) to construct character tables for Lily and Rose with quotes and comments 2) (1) In groups, (P) to discuss and fill in comparison table. 2) Groups to feedback to whole class on whiteboard. 3) (P) to make notes in exercise book 3) 1) (T) to read essay plan with (P). Discuss. 2) (T) to read through essay technique handout (quoting and point, quote, comment) 4) (P) to begin first draft of essay Homework: to complete first draft for Tuesday	1) (P) to watch video and make any notes they feel they need 2) (T) to hand back essays and give general and individual feedback. (P) to use time to see (T) about any confusion and begin to make corrections/amendments	1) (P) to hand in final draft of essay. 2) (T) to introduce S&L assessment. * in groups (P) use drama and getting into role as their character. (P) to devise a scene/conversation between Elizabeth, Lydia, Rose and Lily – 5 mins long* (see additional sheet for criteria) Homework: (P) to make notes on their character 2) (P) to continue with S&L assessment using lesson opportunity to practise 3) Performance of S&L assessment to be recorded using video camera	2) (P) to finish S&L performances. (T) to feedback essay marks, comments. Revision guide
Resources Copies of short story handout		Various handouts, A3 comparison grid, texts	Television/Video, copy of P&P video	Video camera	
Assessment Points (might not be necessary each week)		Formative assessment. Informal monitoring, discussion in pairs, groups and as a whole class, written homework on short story analysis.	Summative assessment – marking of first draft. Informal monitoring	Summative assessment – marking of final draft. Formal assessment. Monitoring of group and whole class. Summative assessment – En 1 activity	Summative assessment – En 1 activity

FIGURE 6.1 EXTRACT FROM AT-A-GLANCE UNIT PLAN – YEAR 10 GCSE WIDER READING COURSEWORK.

CHAPTER SEVEN

Drama in English

KEY FEATURES OF THE AREA OF STUDY

THE RELATIONSHIP BETWEEN DRAMA AND ENGLISH

What is drama?

What is drama in English?

Is there a difference?

This chapter will begin to address these interrelated questions. We all, teachers or not, are likely to make a number of assumptions when we think of what the term 'drama' means to us. Some may immediately associate it with the theatre and the presentation and production of scripted texts. Intending English teachers, from experience of interviewing many, often automatically interpret a question about drama as referring to the literary study of scripts. A glance at the National Curriculum (NC) choice of texts for Reading at KS3 or KS4 tends to support this view, with the range of drama texts being subsumed under 'Literature'; texts to be studied include

- two plays by Shakespeare
- drama by major playwrights
- recent and contemporary drama ... written for young people and adults
- drama ... by major writers from different cultures and traditions.

Examples of authors in each of these categories are provided; they include, in deliberately random sequence, G.B. Shaw, Wole Soyinka, Peter Shaffer, Alan Ayckbourn, R.C. Sherriff, Arthur Miller, Sean O'Casey, Christopher Marlowe, Tennessee Williams, Harold Pinter, Arnold Wesker, Brian Friel and David Hare.

> Which of the above bullet point categories do you think each of these dramatists is placed in, according to the NC? Check your version with the NC; does it raise any issues for you as an English specialist, or as a teacher?

Interestingly, there is a reference in the NC to an implied, potential link between the Drama strand in Speaking and Listening and this literary requirement; the range of drama in En1 at KS3 and KS4 includes the requirement for pupils to engage in 'devising, scripting and performing in plays'. As early as KS2, pupils are expected to script and perform plays.

Returning to the questions posed at the beginning, some people may think first of improvisation and role-play, associated with childhood experiences of experimental early play. It has long been recognized how significant the role of play is in developing young children both as potential learners of the formal curriculum and as social beings. Without entering into complex debates about the socio-cultural differences represented in play, or even attempting a full definition of 'play' beyond the view that it is 'the child's natural ability to use imaginary contexts to make sense of the world' (NATE, 1998: 2), it is nevertheless worth recognizing the amount of research which notes a strong relationship between oral and literacy development where play provides a range of symbolic opportunities to extend children's confident use of both spoken and written language. Nigel Hall and Anne Robinson (1995) and Nigel Hall (1999) have pointed out how literacy materials used in role-play can provide ways for children to understand that reading and writing have important functions.

As far back as 1954, in his book *Child Drama*, in what is now regarded as a seminal work, Peter Slade describes drama as 'born of Play' (1954: 19), including, as starting points, 'games ... free expression ... improvisation'. Although the style of this book now sounds somewhat vague and effusive, based on a romantic notion of drama, nevertheless the connection was established which was an important strategy for drama in education throughout the 1960s and 1970s. The view of drama as 'free expression', as opposed to theatrical skills, is still current. Suzi Clipson-Boyles endorses the position when she says, 'the true spirit of educational drama is about experiences rather than acting' (1998: 122). In a book published in the same year, David Hornbrook, whose name has become synonymous with the tradition of specialist Theatre Studies drama, exposes what he describes as the 'wedge' which Slade drove between the two approaches. He argues that 'drama *does* have its own "body of knowledge made up of theatre crafts, genres and skills", and that this knowledge is as relevant and applicable ... to education in the primary school as it is to sixth-formers' (1998: 56).

THE CURRENT POSITION

Whichever tradition you start from, there are certain features that any intending English teacher nowadays needs to consider:

- Drama is a subject in its own right at GCSE and beyond; according to *All Our Futures* (NACCCE, 1999: 181), it is 'the fastest growing subject [at GCSE] apart from business studies'.

- Drama has an important role throughout the curriculum according to OFSTED, quoted in *All Our Futures*:

The place of drama in the curriculum rests on its inclusion in all three of the Attainment Targets for English in the NC. In addition, drama has a long history as a popular practical artistic subject in its own right. It is also a powerful vehicle for work in a range of subjects, and it contributes to pupils' personal, moral and spiritual development.

(Ibid., 1999: 180)

- Drama is a strand in the NC for English Key Stages 1–4, and thus a statutory requirement. It can do much more than contribute to the Speaking and Listening component; indeed, there are references to drama in some form through all the Attainment Targets at all Key Stages. However, there is evidence that its potential could be more fully recognized. Quoting OFSTED evidence for KSs 1–3, the report says, of drama in English lessons, 'Objectives are unclear, teachers lack confidence in teaching it, and practice varies ... Many secondary [OFSTED] reports make no reference to drama' (Ibid., 1999: 181), though the situation does improve if it is available as a GCSE subject at KS4.

- Drama is explicitly and implicitly encouraged in the National Literacy Strategy, in *Developing Early Writing* (DfEE, 2001e) and the KS3 Framework for Teaching English. See below for more detail.

Many of these references point to the tradition of educational drama as having a key role in contributing to pupils' language development. Also, because of its practical and physical dimension, drama can be a powerful tool for any curriculum area. Howard Gardner, in his work on multiple intelligences (1993), has pointed out how being immersed in an activity in such a way as to involve all the senses makes learning more memorable. Similarly, Phil Race (1993) has shown that 'real people' learn by a mixture of motivation, practice, feedback and reflection.

For the purposes of this chapter, though, I intend to adopt the definition of drama proposed in the Position Paper from the National Association for the Teaching of English (1998) on the subject, namely that drama is the expression of meaning through enactment of events.

> What was your experience of drama at school or beyond? Does it in any way correspond to the definition offered above? Speculate about why that may, or may not, be the case.

DISTINCTIVE FEATURES OF DRAMA IN THE NATIONAL CURRICULUM FOR ENGLISH

As already noted above, the National Curriculum for English identifies a number of specific requirements for Drama. These appear in En1, Speaking and Listening, from KS1 through to KS3 and 4; in En2, Reading in the Literature strand at KS1 through to 3 and 4; and in En3, Writing, from KS2, 3 and 4. At each Key Stage there is reference to improvisation as well as reference to written text and performance.

There is, therefore, not only a statutory requirement for integrating drama into English work, but also enormous scope to do so, now encouraged from the Foundation Stage. The DfEE publication, *Developing Early Writing*, emphasizes throughout that the framework for starting writing begins with 'rich oral experience' (2001e: 7). Introducing ideas and approaches to teaching writing to children in the Reception year, 'The role of oral language … in developing writing' is discussed, with specific reference to teachers to 'encourage re-enacting in drama, dressing-up, converting the role-play area into a bears' cave, a supermarket, and so on' (ibid.: 26). The *National Literacy Strategy* made minimal reference to drama, since acknowledged as an omission and explicitly replaced in the *Key Stage 3 Framework for Teaching English*, which includes subheadings for Speaking,

Listening and Drama in the Teaching Objectives for Years 7, 8 and 9.

Drama can obviously be differentiated from other Speaking and Listening activities by its practical and physical nature. This is both its strength and, occasionally, its limitation, in that teachers sometimes resist drama because the combination of open space, movement, collaboration and speech seems to indicate a potential lack of control. In fact, the opposite is true; drama requires discipline both from those engaged in it as well as those directing it. Problems of management and control are more complex than in the traditional classroom organization and need careful consideration by the experienced as well as the beginning teacher. These issues are raised in more detail in a later section.

Drama can also be powerful in the role it can play in ensuring an inclusive curriculum. The National Curriculum includes a statutory inclusion statement to provide effective learning opportunities for all pupils. Under three principles, it demonstrates how all pupils – boys and girls, pupils with special educational needs, pupils with disabilities, pupils from all social and cultural backgrounds, pupils of different ethnic groups including travellers, refugees and asylum seekers, and those from diverse linguistic backgrounds – should be able to take the advantages offered by the NC. The principles are

1. Setting suitable learning challenges.

2. Responding to pupils' diverse learning needs.

3. Overcoming potential barriers to learning and assessment for individuals and groups of pupils.

It is worth reiterating here that it is important to start by valuing what pupils bring with them rather than seeing diverse needs as problems. Then drama becomes a tool for encouraging participation because it builds on the primary human resource of speaking and it allows the construction of learning contexts which reflect all pupils' lives, interests and experiences. Children's natural inclination to play has been noted above as aiding cognitive and literacy development and described as a starting point for more developed, carefully planned drama activities, especially with literacy needs in mind.

Drama can be fun, inclusive *and* rigorous.

DRAMA IN THE CLASSROOM

It may be easiest for beginning teachers of English (and perhaps for more experienced ones too?) to focus first on the familiar literary text. This section will first explore the way in which a relationship between text and dramatic representations of the text can contribute effectively to pupils' learning, before later looking at ways of approaching scripted and improvised drama.

Working with PGCE trainee English teachers, one of the sessions we devised was to introduce drama in English as required by the NC, and to introduce drama methodology by ensuring that trainees participated in practical drama activities. This approach directly replicates classroom activity and therefore helps trainee teachers in understanding pupils' experiences but, more importantly, it provides the necessary framework for reflection and critical exploration.

The shape of a drama lesson is important, and naturally it requires as much detailed planning as any other English or literacy lesson. We begin by taking the formula of warm-up, or starter, activity (similar to that recommended by the *Framework for English*), followed by the main focus, or exploration, of the lesson, and concluding with a plenary period of relaxation and reflection on the activity and evaluation of their learning. The poem chosen for this session is Jacques Prevert's 'Breakfast' because of its enigmatic qualities.

Presenting this session as a lesson plan (shown on the next page) should help with the task which follows.

Consider the implications for teaching; what might pupils gain from this activity? What would be different if working with, for example, Year 10? In terms of inclusion, how could you ensure that it allowed pupils with SEN and EAL to participate? Where might such an activity occur within a longer unit of work?

The second part of the PGCE drama session focuses on drama to text, or script, raising issues about teaching pupils the distinctive features of writing scripts, as required by the NC. As with any writing activity, the purpose, context and audience will be of prime consideration. All pupils, by the time they reach KS3, should understand the conventions of written playscripts and have engaged with the written genre as well as performing in, and interpreting performances of, possibly, their own written scripts. However, it may well be advisable to revise the format of written scripts by providing a range of short extracts from plays which pupils can examine in order to refresh their knowledge. An effective way of focusing on scripted discourse is to present a very short extract from a television play and compare it to the script. There is an excellent example in the BBC Educational material on *Pride and Prejudice* which has Andrew Davies's

ENGLISH LESSON PLAN   DATE:

TOPIC: Drama

YEAR/ABILITY GROUP: PGCE trainee English teachers   **DURATION:** 1hr 10 mins

LEARNING OBJECTIVES:

All trainees should be able to:

1. Develop their knowledge and understanding of drama in the NC for English
2. Understand drama as a stimulus, as well as a teaching method, for aspects of English
3. Participate in practical drama activities and begin to plan for drama in school

TEACHING AND LEARNING ACTIVITIES

Teaching Activity	Approx. Time	Learning Activity	Approx. Time
Starter: explain learning objectives, on board; explain activity – using drama to interpret a literary text Recap management issues in drama lessons from previous session Divide into groups of four Distribute copies of poem Copy on OHT for reference	10 mins	Record objectives Respond Independent reading of poem	10 mins
Trainees to annotate the poem for key features; highlight verbs; give time limit		Groups discuss and annotate text; do verbs reveal key points?	5 mins
Each group to dramatize the poem as they choose, to reveal their interpretation for presentation Monitor without intervention		Work on dramatization	25 mins
Discuss evaluation criteria; Presentations of dramatizations	5 mins	Watch presentations; make notes according to agreed evaluation criteria	20 mins
Plenary: guide discussion of interpretations presented Trainees to note learning points Return to objectives to focus learning		Discussion Notes recorded	10 mins

DIFFERENTIATED SUPPORT (e.g. your plans for SEN, EAL etc.): n/a
ICT USE: OHP
ASSESSMENT OPPORTUNITY: what opportunities would there be for assessment?
– for discussion in the next session
HOMEWORK: for next session, prepare a rationale and plan for teaching a similar
text to a class
RESOURCES: copies of poem/OHP/poem on OHT

script for the opening sequence alongside the actual opening of the popular 1995 television version. (To take this a stage further, you could compare the opening of the television version with that of the novel. That would potentially provoke a lively and revealing analysis of different genres and media.)

The process of moving from improvisation to script, as exemplified from the PGCE course drama session, could also be used with small groups working on various aspects of a possible 'play', perhaps for performance to a peer group assembly, or initially just to the rest of the class.

Before writing is embarked on, certain aspects of written composition need explicit consideration, since writing script is very different from other written discourse. Each of these points needs some investigation with the pupils, but the depth and extent of examination would depend on the pupils' age, abilities and experience. Consider:

- how spoken, scripted language differs from ordinary conversation; taped real language events are helpful to show how spoken and written discourse differ – even a short transcript demonstrates how real, spontaneous speech is marked by hesitation, repetition, incompleteness, reliance on gesture and intonation and the social context in which it occurs

- how spoken, scripted language differs from other written genres with which pupils are familiar. For those who are less familiar or secure with scripts, a writing frame which models the first few lines could provide a starting point

- who will form the audience for this piece

- the information necessary for the audience to understand the plot, and how that information can best be conveyed – examining two opening scenes of plays which do this effectively and economically will help, e.g., Shaw's *Pygmalion*, John Godber's *Teechers* (sic)

■ how much explicit direction the writer should provide,
e.g., look at Shaw's or Arthur Miller's directions, compared
to Shakespeare's famous 'Exit pursued by a bear' in *A
Winter's Tale.*

An analysis of techniques used during improvisations could provide fruitful material for several of the above points.

DRAMA AND WRITING

Drama not only acts as a starting point for writing scripts, but can also provide a context for other writing activities. Ideas for explorations of writing derived from, or linked to, drama are frequent in the texts referred to in this chapter's bibliography. In an article in *The Secondary English Magazine*, Teresa Grainger offers a list of writing opportunities based on drama conventions 'which … can lead pupils to refine the form and enrich the content of writing linked to the texts they study' (2002: 16).

Working in a fictionalized situation, pupils will find that audience and purpose are immediately supplied by the context. For example, in the Urbania project referred to in the previous chapter, writing letters of protest or support, producing leaflets, writing scripts for news bulletins, reports on the feasibility of the project as well as newspaper reports and features would all be appropriate non-fiction texts to create. Pupils can engage in fictional genres by writing in role, where characters present their points of view in a hot-seat activity, followed by thoughtful diary entries exploring the characters' reasons for arriving at these views. Such writing could help to counteract a possible tendency for the characters to become stereotyped or merely reactionary. If the pupils have engaged with the activity, their motivation to produce writing as a natural outcome is often enhanced.

A case study of a trainee teacher's approach to using drama as a means of improving pupils' persuasive writing deserves attention here.

CASE STUDY: AN INVESTIGATION INTO THE EFFECTIVENESS OF DRAMA-BASED TEACHING STRATEGIES ON PUPILS' WRITING

As part of the exploration of curriculum development, one trainee from the English group, Matthew, chose the above title as the focus for his investigation. The data was gathered from a high-achieving Year 9 class in a mixed,

11–16 comprehensive school in an urban, ethnically diverse community.

As part of his second school placement, Matthew had been revising key scenes in *Macbeth* during February and April 2002 to prepare the pupils for their KS3 SATs. He had noticed how the pupils 'very much enjoyed the drama approaches we made to the text'. He had also noticed that pupils' writing often lacked cohesion, beginning well but with less successful endings. Therefore, it seemed a logical step to use drama strategies to try to improve their writing, specifically concentrating on persuasive writing. In his rationale for his choice of investigation, Matthew considered the advantages of drama as a means of motivating pupils, asking the question: 'Why use drama to teach writing?' Three clear reasons are given, summarized here for brevity:

- the experiential nature of play as a means of interacting with the world, with subsequent learning benefits

- by giving primacy to spoken language, linguistic repertoires can be enhanced; quoting Neelands, Matthew explains how drama can operate reciprocally along a continuum: 'Just as working in drama can help students to turn abstract ideas and written language into concrete and living representations, so it can help students to translate lived experience into a variety of written representations' (Neelands, 1998: 2)

- in Matthew's words, drama allows 'varied, challenging, motivational' social interaction, important for beginning to articulate unformed thoughts and ideas, and for testing these out in a 'safe' environment; it also frees the teacher to become a player alongside the pupils.

THE LESSONS

Over a course of six lessons, including several homework tasks, Matthew began by asking pupils to respond instantly to questions about 'loves and hates'; they then worked with response partners to try to persuade each other into doing something they were reluctant to do. Scenarios were provided, such as 'You have seen something very expensive and you try to persuade someone to buy it for you.' Selected pairs performed their role-plays, with the onlookers noting the use of language techniques. Using these notes, Matthew produced a 'Language of Persuasion' support and reference sheet, which was used for pupils to check how many techniques they had employed in a short written piece based on their role-plays.

The whole class then watched a video extract from *Room 101*, a television programme deriving its title from Room 101 in Orwell's *1984*, in which guests attempt to persuade the host to banish items they hate into the oblivion of Room 101. With the help of a simple tick-sheet, the pupils noted how many persuasive techniques were used during the extract. They were to spot such techniques as: exclamation/comparison/imperatives/ hyperbole/rhetoric/facts/alliteration/emotive language/rhyme/repetition.

The pupils then began work in groups on their own *Room 101* programme, attempting to use as many of the persuasive devices as they could. Presentations of the eventual interviews were recorded on video with short discussions to reach consensus about whether the items should be con-signed to Room 101. In order to reflect on each other's presentations, with a view to later improvement, the pupils used the same tick-sheet as when they watched the 'real' programme extract.

As a means of summative assessment, the pupils were asked to write an individual persuasive piece either based on their *Room 101* presentation or anything else they were interested in.

For the assignment purposes, Matthew concentrated on three pupils. He compared their persuasive writing before the drama activity with the sum-mative piece set at the end of the revision programme. His findings were:

> All pupils have extended the vocabulary of their emotive language and all have included some kind of factual, statistical evidence. Rhetoric is evident, particularly three-pronged rhetoric, which pupils seemed to enjoy playing with. The playfulness of the language is another factor to be taken into con-sideration; puns, alliteration have been attempted in some cases very suc-cessfully … Finally, every piece is much more cohesive, some ending with even more punch than they began, and structured to include almost all of the persuasive techniques they were taught.

The conclusion of his investigation examines critically his own learning from the experience. Besides analysing his learning in relation to his professional development, he emphasizes how much he enjoyed the unit, 'approaching lessons with a great deal of enthusiasm'. His concluding sentence reads: 'The fact is that lessons were a lot of fun, we all enjoyed playing.'

MANAGING DRAMA

English teachers sometimes feel less confident about incorporating drama into their lessons because of the perceived difficulties of managing an unfa-miliar situation. Often, these perceptions are unfounded, not least because most pupils regard drama as an enjoyable, memorable and hence motivat-ing experience. This is usually the case in schools where:

- there is an established tradition of successful drama (and not just the school play)

- talk is perceived is an important dimension of learning

- there is a genuine commitment to the development of oracy

- these issues have been discussed by staff and not merely formulated as disembodied management policies.

That does not mean that drama should be avoided if these conditions are not present. If children do not respond enthusiastically or, indeed, if they respond too enthusiastically to drama, there are usually good reasons. These might include unclear aims in planning, resulting in the purpose of the activity being unclear, unclear instructions, and tasks which are too complicated or not sufficiently challenging, so that drama begins to seem mere 'playing'. All these can be avoided by paying attention to the links between planning and management; by considering carefully beforehand where moments of tension or conflict might arise – as they should in an effective drama lesson – and planning appropriate interventions in order to manage them.

Teachers should always be prepared to explain and justify why they are doing what they are doing – to other teachers, to pupils, to parents and certainly to themselves. Clarity of thinking about the value of drama as a learning process, at both theoretical and practical levels, is necessary. Careful planning for drama activities, using appropriately selected techniques, will reinforce confident management of drama lessons.

> Return to the previous chapter on Oracy. Read through the Urbania project and, using the *planning template*, create a plan for a drama lesson, incorporating outcomes with reference to NC Speaking and Listening at KS3 and 4.

The task on planning is a difficult one, not because planning for drama is significantly different from any other curriculum planning, but because there are issues related to planning without a context which reduce it to a paper exercise rather than a carefully thought out stage in real pupils' learning. However, we wanted to include such a task in order to reinforce the links between planning and managing. As you attempt the task, 'walk through' it with a specific class in mind, examining at each step implications for management. The next sections on 'Defining boundaries' and 'Drama techniques' should help your deliberations.

There are also wider issues about planning which caution against a single format, automatically applied. Rigid adherence to a particular model (for example, that provided by the KS3 Framework) may limit possibilities for learning instead of expanding them, besides becoming somewhat routine and potentially repetitive. This is especially true for drama lessons where it is arguable that the teacher needs to be responsive to immediate developments which may not have been planned but which can be thoughtfully evaluated and critically examined afterwards.

That said, it is necessary to begin somewhere, preferably somewhere secure. Beginning teachers certainly need a model to adopt and follow until they have enough experience to critique and amend it. The model offered in this book has been arrived at after long deliberation, bearing in mind that those inducting beginning teachers have a responsibility to ensure their familiarity with recommended or statutory requirements for planning. So, stick with the template for the time being, and at a later stage, consider whether it meets the needs of drama work.

A new teacher, however, may feel understandably more reluctant to use drama activities without some previous advice. So, besides offering a clear rationale for the activity, careful planning and preparation can pre-empt and prevent behaviour problems arising.

■ DEFINE BOUNDARIES

Some rules of conduct are necessary, though they are best kept simple, for example:

- Have an agreed signal at which everyone stops: two claps/a whistle/a raised arm/'Stop!', etc. – explain that it is really important for safety reasons.
- The signal can be incorporated into the drama: 'At the signal, I want to see who can freeze fastest and hold the freeze best.'
- Avoid physical contact. Some pupils will turn any situation into physical conflict. Explain and demonstrate how actors mime fights. Have a non-negotiable sanction for anyone infringing the rule.
- Define the space available, how it can and cannot be used, integrating purposefully into the drama.
- Noise levels may be a problem if other lessons would be disturbed. Making mime, whispering or silent movie style

a major focus can provide temporary respite, but it is important to discuss the issue with other teachers so they appreciate that noise does not mean loss of control.

WORKING SPACE

The ideal space is probably a drama studio, if available, though systems for booking and using them may require prior organization. As in every aspect of teaching, attention paid to prior organization helps to ensure smooth, calm operations, so trouble taken in advance is usually well invested. Failing that, any safe, open space is enough. The classroom can be perfectly accept-able, with chairs and tables moved aside, or incorporated into the drama (the teacher's desk can represent a position of authority and become a focus for acting out power relationships). An inexperienced teacher, however, will need to plan carefully in advance how to manage furniture removal!

DRAMA TECHNIQUES

Through drama activities, a rich variety of the different contexts of all lan-guage modes can be explored. Familiar drama techniques are listed below, drawn from many sources (see, for example, Heathcote and Wagner, 1999, and Neelands, 2000). This is certainly not an exhaustive list but should provide a starting point for exploration:

- mime: movement, gesture and expression without words
- improvisation: enacting a scenario spontaneously
- role-play: adopting the role of a different person, real or imaginary
- hot seating: questions are posed to a character in role
- freeze-frames or tableaux: moments captured and 'frozen'
- thought tracking: speaking aloud the inner thoughts of a character, sometimes contrasting with what is actually spoken
- sound tracking: using sounds to enhance atmosphere or events
- forum theatre: pupils form the audience and offer ideas at critical moments about the drama they are watching so as to influence its direction
- vox pop: edited version of 'person in the street' interview
- casting director: deciding on the appropriate actor for particular characters

- role-on-the-wall: enlarged character outline posted on the wall for pupils to annotate by writing key words or phrases.

Finally, teacher in role should be mentioned. This is a more challenging technique or dimension of drama teaching but when used appropriately, it can be a particularly powerful resource, as well as a means of guiding and managing the drama from within the action. The teacher enters into the improvisation as an equal participant, potentially enhancing the experience for the pupils. The benefits of this technique include:

- making the imaginary situation more authentic
- the teacher is able to model language, make appropriate responses and raise questions
- it allows the teacher to disrupt the predictable response and create new directions
- it challenges the norm of pupil–teacher relationships.

PROGRESSION AND ASSESSMENT OF DRAMA IN ENGLISH

The principles of assessment apply as much to drama as any other area of the curriculum:

- Assessment is integral to planning for clear, achievable learning objectives.
- Assessment focuses clearly on agreed targets between learner and teacher.
- Assessment creates challenges and is responsive to individual needs.

What is specific to drama work in the English curriculum, though, that teachers may be assessing? One answer is to refer to the statutory requirements of the NC, track through the references to drama and ensure that these are not only covered within planning units, but are also formatively assessed and recorded to show pupils' progress (or not, as the case may be). Bunyan et al. (2000) acknowledge that progression in drama, as in oracy, is harder to define than in reading or writing; after all, it is evident from the written product how much a pupil can, for instance, use a variety of sentence types to create particular effects.

In drama work, it is especially important, therefore, to have clear learning objectives. It is also important to remember that progress and progression are not the same; progress is to do with an individual pupil's development, whereas progression is more about the teacher's deliberate attempts to plan for activities which provide evidence of broadening, deepening and strengthening pupils' skills, knowledge and understanding.

Cracking Drama (Bunyan et al., 2000) deals helpfully with precisely these issues of progression and assessment. The authors demonstrate the complexity of progression, envisaging it as strands of interwoven ribbon drawing on Bruner's spiral curriculum. They tease out the strands of 'engagement, critical analysis and transference' as applied specifically to drama in English, showing how teacher intervention within the drama (teacher in role), between imagined and real worlds (teacher in usual teacher role), and beyond the drama (transferring learning), is central to their view of progression.

Techniques for assessing drama in English are again underpinned by the same principles that hold good for any subject – notably observation and questioning. The significant question for the teacher here is: 'What learning activities am I providing that will help me measure the pupils' progress in English, through drama?' An interesting response to this question is offered in the case study in the oracy chapter, where a beginning teacher begins to integrate drama into her unit of work in order to develop the pupils' speaking and listening skills which are being assessed for GCSE.

TEACHING SHAKESPEARE'S PLAYS

No chapter on Drama in the English curriculum could omit attention to Shakespeare's plays. Arguments about their validity in the school curriculum centre on debates about the traditional canon of English Literature and the ways in which recent critical perspectives interpret the plays, alongside an assumption that traditional approaches to teaching Shakespeare's plays tend to put pupils off engaging with theatrical experiences rather than encouraging them. These arguments are well summarized by Rex Gibson in his excellent *Teaching Shakespeare* (1998: 27–8). Gibson and his work for the Shakespeare in Schools Project has done more to provide teachers with a broad, theoretically eclectic – and well-informed – but primarily active and comprehensive approach to the plays than any other we know. It is certainly true that the question 'Why teach Shakespeare?' is often best countered with 'Why not?', though Gibson provides a more thoughtful rationale under four headings:

- abiding and familiar concerns: relationships between individuals and their societies retain significance and meaning, capable of reinterpretation for different generations

- pupil development: studying the plays helps develop emotional intelligence

- language: its power is enriching when carefully explored

- otherness: the strange, unfamiliar and fantastic imagination that created the plays (Gibson, 1998: 2).

Importantly, for intending teachers, the pedagogy Gibson promotes places the plays as dramatic devices at the heart of teaching Shakespeare. Perhaps the biggest disservice to the playwright is to treat plays as texts to be mined for sequences of metaphors and given line-by-line explanation rather than engaged in as scripts to be played with – irreverently if necessary.

His final comment is:

> Shakespeare remains a genius of outstanding significance in the development of English language, literature and drama. All students should have opportunities through practical experience, to make up their own minds about what Shakespeare might hold for them.
>
> **(Gibson, 1998: 6)**

Whatever the arguments about Shakespeare's place in the English curriculum, they have not polarized, and should thus continue to engender healthy debate. Nevertheless, a Shakespeare play is compulsory study at KS3 and KS4, and is encouraged by the NLS in Year 6, where the Range of Study specifies 'drama by long-established authors including, where appropriate, study of a Shakespeare play'.

■ AN APPROACH TO TEACHING *THE TEMPEST*

This session is loosely adapted from a Unit of Work on *The Tempest* (Gibson, 1995), devised by a former trainee teacher and originally intended for a Year 7 mixed-ability class. It could be readily adapted to a range of ages and levels, as most of the activities described in this chapter can. It is based on principles which are briefly summarized below, some of which are shared with those outlined by Rex Gibson (1998) in *Teaching Shakespeare*, but which we have also arrived at over thirty years of teaching the plays.

PRINCIPLES

- Know what you as teacher think about this play, without relying on received opinion but approaching it anew because you need to.

■ Think about where your pupils are starting from, and try to address some of the myths (such as 'Shakespeare's boring') through pupils' active involvement.

■ Use collaborative, co-operative strategies, as would happen with a theatre group (see, for example, Berry, 1993).

■ Treat the plays as scripts; they are dramas intended for public performance.

■ Physicalize the text, exploiting the way the language is often performative.

■ Enjoy yourselves.

STRUCTURE

The structure follows that of a classic drama lesson and is, indeed, similar to that of literacy lessons, in that it has a warm-up, followed by a more detailed exploration and ending with reflection and evaluation.

PROCEDURE

Ensure that there is adequate space for comfortable movement. Do not give the play's title or mention Shakespeare if you can avoid it; treat it as a drama session. Whoever is leading the session needs a confident familiarity with the play.

WARM-UP

■ Begin by showing an OHT or enlarged picture of a seventeenth-century sailing ship with a mind-mapping activity about what the ship was like; what conditions were like on board; who might travel on it and why, etc. Include a question about the sailors' tasks. The questions, and the extent of the teacher's guidance, can be adapted according to the age of the pupils or students.

■ Move into a suitable space and ask for mimes of sailors' activities on board such a sailing ship; encourage as wide a range as possible while retaining the movement of the sea.

■ Move into pairs to continue and develop the mime. What happens to their movements if a storm is brewing? Bring fear and desperation into the tasks, with accompanying music or sound effects if possible, culminating in the crescendo of a final wreck.

INTRODUCTION

- Relax; the teacher in role as a narrator could develop the story that a king and courtiers are aboard the ship. Consider questions of authority and hierarchy on board the ship. Some further improvisation of the king talking to the sailors and the ship's captain about the voyage and a possible approaching storm would help to establish the context.

- Distribute numbered lines, one per pair, taken from the play's opening scene but omitting much of the detail as well as speakers' names; it is important to introduce the actual language though. The first few lines, of 12 altogether, are provided to give a flavour of the task:

  1. Fall to't yarely, or we run aground, bestir, bestir.

  2. Yare yare: take in the topsail.

  3. I pray you now keep below.

  4. You mar our labour, keep your cabins.

  (Admittedly, the selection loses Sebastian's and Antonio's violent cursing and Gonzalo's more conciliatory manner but we think that this is less important than some physical involvement in the shipwreck which sets the emotional context for the development of the play.)

- The pairs speculate about who might speak the line (sailor/king/captain/courtier) and how it is spoken; lines to be practised aloud, they are short enough to be committed to memory.

- Movement of mimes, encroaching storm with sound effects and the lines spoken in order are orchestrated to indicate the end of Act I sc1.

- Ideally, with more time, the next stage would be to return to the scene and read it in small groups.

FOLLOWING THE SHIPWRECK; EXPLORATION ACTIVITY

- In small groups, provided with large sheets of sugar paper and crayons, create a version of the island on which all the passengers have, separately, been washed ashore. Identify certain features of the island:

a cave

a wood of pine trees

solitary pine tree

beaches

shipwrecked boat

a dwelling.

■ Teacher or leader to tell the story which Prospero tells Miranda, Act I sc2, (including the rescue of Ariel).

■ Learning more about the island; choric speaking of Caliban's speech, Act III sc2, 'Be not afeared, the isle is full of noises'.

■ Distribute numbered lines of speech, broken according to punctuation to make sense, shared between pairs or small groups.

■ All walk in a circle, trying the lines aloud, experimenting with tone and mood.

■ Stand still and whisper lines.

■ In a circle, stand in numbered order of lines (16).

■ Speak the lines in sequence; repeat to create mood, using music and turning off the lights.

■ Discuss what picture of the island is emerging, then return to Caliban's story, Act I sc2 lines 320–76 (copies of this short extract should be available to small groups).

REFLECTION/EVALUATION

■ Stress that this is an *approach* to the play, it is only the beginning of establishing tentative exploration, focusing first on the plot and some magical aspects of the play.

■ Analyse what each stage of the session was trying to achieve.

■ Read Carol Ann Duffy's poem 'Anne Hathaway' in *The World's Wife* (Duffy, 1999) as a commentary on Shakespeare

Which principles, outlined above, were exemplified in the session? How/what did they achieve?

Look at the references to drama in NC for KS3 and KS4; which were covered?

Read the poem cited above; what possibilities for further exploration does it present?

Returning to the questions posed at the beginning of the chapter, we may not have answered them conclusively but we hope we have identified some of the complexities they raise. We have attempted to place them in a context which encourages beginning teachers to explore them further, both as elements in the intellectual process of professional development and in practical terms, in the classroom and drama studio.

KEY TEXTS

Bunyan, P. et al. (2000) *Cracking Drama: Progression in Drama within English (5–16)*. Sheffield: NATE.

Gibson, R. (1998) *Teaching Shakespeare*. Cambridge: Cambridge University Press.

Neelands, J. (1998) *Beginning Drama 11–14*. London: David Fulton.

Neelands, J. (2000) *Structuring Drama Work*. Cambridge: Cambridge University Press.

CHAPTER EIGHT

Media in English

INTRODUCTION

Media Studies as an aspect of English continues to be one of the most exciting as well as one of the most hotly contested areas for teaching and learning. In essence, the debate rages around what kinds of influences Media Studies should be allowed to have on the rest of the subject area called English – indeed, whether it ought to be part of English at all.

WHAT IS IN A NAME?

But first there is the issue of what to call it. The National Curriculum for English refers to 'the media', 'media and moving image texts', 'media products' and 'electronic media'. On that evidence, the National Curriculum uses the term 'the media' much as one does in ordinary speech or writing, that is, to mean a collection of ways of communicating with people that usually includes newspapers and magazines, advertising in all its manifestations, films/videos/DVDs, television and radio, and an assortment of leaflets and pamphlets for a variety of purposes.

Latterly, the Internet and the World Wide Web have been included in the list, as these recent additions to the media have also generated a distinctive range of means of communication.

In the world of higher education, the term 'Media Studies' seems to be preferred, and that is the title also of a GCSE and a GCE A level course. So, when the study of the media is perceived as a separate entity, the term

'Media Studies' seems to be used. When it is part of the subject English, 'studying the Media' seems to help make that distinction.

The wrangle over what to call it is no mere arcane discussion, but rather goes to the heart of the 'problem' with the status of studying the Media in educational contexts. It will help to see that debate in a brief historical context.

MEDIA STUDIES MEETS ENGLISH: SOME KEY CONSIDERATIONS

Media Studies traces its origins to Film Studies courses in universities that started to appear in the late 1960s and early 1970s in the USA and the UK. The argument was that films contain many similarities with literary texts, as well as exhibiting distinctive features of their own:

- They can be grouped in genres.
- They use features of narrative which are similar to written texts.
- They have characters, brought to life by actors.
- It is possible to make qualitative judgements – some films are better than others, some films are more successful with audiences than others.
- It is possible to make aesthetic judgements about aspects of film, especially in the area of photography and filming techniques.
- There are 'canonical films'.
- Films and film makers influence and are influenced by each other, and intertextual references are common.
- Films are sold as products – they are advertised, there is a 'star system', we watch trailers.
- There is a 'film industry', with big players, big companies sometimes making big profits. There are films that cost millions of dollars/pounds to make, with all the trappings of economic enterprise.
- Films require distinctive processes in creating the final product, i.e., the film that is shown on the cinema screen – the entire editing process, including sequencing, selection of scenes, adding music. It is also possible to have more than one version of the same film, for different audiences/markets, or the so-called 'director's cut' version.

Please notice that what the list attempts to do is present a sequence that starts with criteria that are clearly derived from the world of literary criticism, and then moves to a set of distinctive criteria that is only ever applied to film.

In that comment lies the perceived challenge to the scholarly world of literary study – not only were academics interested in giving film academic respectability, but they were also asking searching questions such as what would become of our view of literary texts if we subjected them to the kinds of analysis habitually used for film?

And that is what happened. Some people had the temerity, as it was perceived, to demystify literary texts, and see them as products rather than 'inspired artistic creations' or 'the products of geniuses'. As an example, it is viable to regard literary texts as the outcomes of a sequence of choices, just as film can be. Writers are in charge of such choices as: names of characters; settings and locations; historical period; genre; narrative sequence and events; the ending. A stylistic approach to authorial choices would even consider relevant selections by the writer/creator at sentence and word level.

Not only are texts the products of choices, they are also produced and consumed at particular times and in particular places. We habitually talk about 'Nineteenth-century literature' or 'American literature', with the implication that texts from that specific era or geographical location possess distinctive features in large part derived from their date of writing and initial reading, or from the part of the world where they were written and first read. In that sense, 'great literature' can be taken as being as much a part of the wider cultural scene as newspapers, television, advertisements and the cinema.

THE CHALLENGE OF CULTURAL STUDIES

Out of those considerations, Cultural Studies was born. As a distinctive academic field, it draws on a number of other disciplines to describe, explore, and critique manifestations of the culture in which we live (contemporary) or the culture of past times (historical). For example:

- it uses terms more usually associated with economics (production, consumption, media institutions) to examine the 'culture industry', as in films, or television, or newspaper dynasties, or book publishing houses

- it uses sociological terms when exploring the differences between 'high culture' and 'popular culture' (working-class texts, television viewing figures by social class).

However, it also makes use of many skills refined in the practice of literary criticism, but applies them to all sorts and conditions of texts, in an attempt to describe and demystify the practices of journalists, leader writers, advertisers, propagandists – to name but a small selection from the available areas of study.

We have to remember that the world of literary criticism had been dominated for many years by a set of views that prioritized 'high culture' above all other manifestations of 'culture'. The literary debates in those circles revolved around identifying the great writers and the great texts. In addition, that view made claims about the civilizing effects of exposure to great literature, with associated views about how literature provides access to 'wisdom', somewhat vaguely defined. If that could be done, then, according to that argument, readers can be directed to the best that has been written and said for their edification and general spiritual and moral benefit – the so-called liberal humanist tradition. That viewpoint is widely contested, but at the same time it is still very much alive. For example, as recently as 2003, the Prince of Wales, in an article in the Royal Society of Literature's magazine, commented on the need for 'a return to a traditional curriculum centred on Shakespeare and the classics of English literature' (as quoted in the *Times Educational Supplement*, 30 January 2003).

Out of that highly influential academic tradition came the notion of the literary canon, that list of writers universally acknowledged to be the finest in the language. Now is not the time to debate fully the notion of a literary canon – for further consideration of it, please see Chapter 5. For the moment, it suffices to say that the high-culture view of certain, predominantly literary, texts was challenged by the founders of the Cultural Studies movement.

The result was that a tradition in literary criticism was challenged, and a new and distinctive set of ideas was brought to bear on a discrete yet much more widely inclusive set of texts drawn from a variety of media. Culture in this definition is defined more in terms of the range and variety of textual manifestations, rather than in any subset perceived to be more culturally important.

THE FOCUS ON 'TEXT'

Let us be clear: it is true that a soap opera is as much a 'text' as a Shakespeare play. It is also true to say that they share many similarities as well as having distinctive differences, textually as well as in their modes of production and consumption. A Cultural Studies advocate would say that those statements are worthy of further exploration, analysis and theorizing.

The results could be:

- a deeper understanding of the general cultural and historical context for Shakespeare's plays

- an awareness that Shakespeare had to write to live, and that success was important to him economically and politically

- some insights into the effects of the social mix in Shakespeare's theatre on the structure and content of his plays

- perceptions about how contemporary soap operas have to tackle those very same issues.

In addition, admittedly somewhat perversely, it is possible to take a 'high-culture' view of a soap opera, in the sense that:

- soap operas traditionally deal with moral and controversial issues, thus possessing the potential to influence (possibly for the better) the lives of the viewers

- we could make some qualitative judgements between soap operas: which is the best, and why?

But you will also see that this attempt is somewhat fraught, given that the acknowledgement of the pervasive impact and influence of soap operas would prove a sticking point with most advocates of high-cultural superiority.

On the other hand, what has happened in the development of Media Studies in schools is that teachers and other advocates for this approach have pushed the boundaries even further by seeing what happens in terms of teaching and learning when we apply Cultural Studies criteria to a Shakespeare play, and sometimes Liberal Humanist literary critical approaches to a soap opera, as exemplified above. In the end, the cross-fertilization of ideas has proved very illuminating of both Shakespeare and soap opera.

But it also has to be reported that as well as cross-fertilization, there has been a strong element of difference, so that Media Studies has come to be seen as a distinctive and different aspect of English, and given the intellectual schisms of the past, it is no wonder that in the end aspects of distinctiveness and difference are more apparent than the healing balm of open-minded exchanges of ideologies.

The above is a very condensed presentation of the history and issues. Some would also call it somewhat partial, but the intention was to be fair. To check out the degree of fairness or fuller explorations of the history and issues, please consult:

- chapter 3 of Masterman (1985): one of the founding fathers of Media Education, and a seminal text, despite its age

- chapter 7 of Buckingham and Sefton-Green (1994), a chapter that also argues for the distinctiveness of Media Education in the curriculum

- chapters 1 and 10 of Buckingham (1990), which are also very interesting for their combining of pedagogical issues with historical and distinctive features of Media Education

- Brereton (2001) for an up-to-date glossary of terms and general reference guide, with useful bibliographies by topic – look up 'cultural studies', for example, for a helpful working definition and good reading list.

PAUSE

There is a lot to ponder in the above. The following prompts are intended to make you think through some of the ideas and concepts summarized so far.

- How would you define your attitude to Media Studies before reading the start of this chapter?

- How have your views changed so far?

- What do you find particularly controversial about this chapter so far?

- What experience(s) of Media, Media Studies, and/or Media in English do you bring to the reading of this chapter?

- At the moment, where do you position yourself in the debate between a cultural heritage view of English and the cultural analysis view?

- Are you beginning to see any attractions in incorporating aspects of Media Studies into your teaching of English?

MEDIA IN ENGLISH CLASSROOMS: MAPPING THE TERRITORY

Media Studies has, for some people, become synonymous with sloppy thinking, unchallenging intellectual material and a lack of academic rigour. Keep your eyes open for Media Studies mentioned, for example, when someone wants to criticize some of the areas for study in some modern degree courses.

These critics of Media Studies usually come from people who (deliberately) misunderstand or fail to acknowledge the intellectual basis for the subject. Media Studies has to be demonized because it presents a threat to a preferred (in their view) set of ideological imperatives. At bottom, there is a fear that if 'great literature', for example, is demystified (and seen as the outcome of a process of production), then something very important will be lost. What those critics fail to see – or rather do not want to admit that they see – is that in demystifying literature we make its consumption (reading) and its creation (writing) much more accessible to all sorts and conditions of pupils.

So, the argument presented here states that, far from being intellectually unchallenging, Media Studies brings a distinctive set of emphases to bear on the notion of text, of whatever kind. Much analysis of media texts draws very effectively on notions of:

- representation – how are particular groups/individuals/issues presented?
- audience – who is it aimed at? Why?
- ideology – what set of values are implied, promulgated?
- language – what distinctive aspects of the choice of medium are used? How? Why?

Len Masterman is credited with giving the study of Media intellectual and pedagogic respectability. His definition is as follows:

> Media education *necessarily* assumes that [media] experiences are reconstructed, represented, (re-presented), packaged and shaped in identifiable and characteristic forms by media institutions, media technologies and the practices of media professionals.
>
> (Masterman, 1985: 21)

In the 1990s, the British Film Institute produced a curriculum statement for secondary Media Education (BFI, 1991) in an attempt to define the distinctiveness of the subject. Andrew Goodwyn echoes that document's conclusions when he defines six key areas in Media Education as:

- Agencies: who is communicating and why?
- Categories: what kind of text is it?
- Technologies: how is it produced?
- Languages: how do we know what it means?
- Audiences: who receives it, and what sense do they make of it?
- Representations: how does it present its subject(s)? (1992: 48–53)

Buckingham and Sefton-Green go even further when they write that:

> English is defined in terms of a set of practices – reading, writing, speaking and listening … Media Studies, by contrast, is defined in terms of a set of concepts – media language (or 'forms and conventions'), representation, institution and audience.
>
> (1994: 132–3)

It is possible to take issue with Buckingham and Sefton-Green's view of English as a 'set of practices', but they add to our understanding of what constitutes Media in English, and it is possible to argue that a variety of academics and commentators have articulated a set of concepts that have a lot of elements in common.

So we can say with some certainty and confidence that rather than being an intellectually sloppy and badly defined academic domain, the study of the Media springs from a rigorously articulated and intellectually robust set of informing concepts. It therefore follows that if we are to enable our learners to understand the effects and influences of the texts that are most likely to have impact on them, we cannot ignore working with a range of texts other than literary ones.

As has become the pattern in this book, here are some thoughts and suggestions for how studying the Media can contribute to teaching and learning in the Attainment Targets (ATs) for English. There are no separate ATs for Media. However, media texts provide us with a very varied resource to draw on as we enable learners to make progress in the ATs. Media also provides opportunities for cultural analysis, both contemporary and historical, as well as offering interesting possibilities for practical applications of understandings, including the use of ICT.

MEDIA AND SPEAKING AND LISTENING

The spoken word is a vibrant aspect of the media output of the contemporary world. There are many opportunities to explore examples, with a view to using that analysis for practical application and replication:

- Radio is a rich resource of genres – including soap opera.
- Radio advertisements have distinguishing features.
- The uses of sound on the Internet are worth investigating.
- Recording and editing sound digitally is very straightforward using computers.

- Exploration of the variety of accents heard during a day's television or radio.

- A school radio station.

Oral activities within a Media Unit of Study could include:

- preparing and delivering a group presentation to a commissioning editor for a new soap opera or a new kind of community radio station

- preparing and performing a radio news bulletin

- recording a radio programme of another distinctive kind

- presenting plans to a company for an advertising campaign.

At the same time as learners demonstrate competence and progress in aspects of Speaking and Listening, they can also reflect on and write about the media specific aspects of their study.

MEDIA AND READING

Enabling learners to become self-aware readers of visual texts ranks as an important development in the reading skills of teenagers. In secondary schools, we can use the Media focus to significantly enhance our learners as readers. In that process, we will have to provide learners with access to the appropriate metalanguage, and some terminology will have to be introduced; for example, learners will need to know about the range of film/television camera shots and the effects they create. In that sense, we are addressing the grammar of Media language, much in the same way as we approach the study of written and spoken language, through exploration and description, and at the same time recognizing the need to be able to use appropriate terminology.

Visual literacy is very important, given the importance assigned to it by all sorts and conditions of communicators constantly around us, from advertisers to political parties. Then there are those distinctive kinds of texts that incorporate words and pictures:

- graphical novels

- photostories.

There are resources available that enable learners to explore the impact of:

- picture sequencing
- picture cropping
- adding a new soundtrack to a piece of film
- changing the voice-over commentary.

In other words, learners can experience aspects of making choices in the creative process of making news or feature film that have important impacts on how meanings are made from the text.

All those activities have the potential to develop learners' reading skills in the area of visual media. There will need to be moments when learners can explicitly talk and write about the skills they have been using; it is important for both teachers and learners that the connections between a print-based view of reading and a moving image view of reading are made explicit. As teachers, we need to recognize our expertise in reading printed texts, while at the same time making the necessary adjustments when reading a different medium. Pupils need to see that making meanings from moving image texts is very similar to making meanings from printed ones – it is all about making meanings from texts and being able to articulate how those meanings emerge.

MEDIA AND WRITING

Media study provides opportunities for the development and consolidation of previously encountered forms of writing. But here it is important to see that work in Media can extend learners' and teachers' views of writing, in terms of the process and possible products.

It is perfectly possible to argue that creating a media text is a process of writing, taken in the broadest sense. Therefore, it is viable to consider, for example, creating a radio programme as a writing activity. It will require learners to use a range of 'traditional' writing styles in the process of completing the task, as well as providing opportunities for the participants to identify the distinctive aspects of 'writing in the media'.

The ability to create visual texts opens up exciting possibilities for reconsidering the writing process and what constitutes 'writing' when operating with pictures, on film, in a cartoon, or on the printed page. With that very much in mind, it is appropriate to consider the impact of using a variety of technologies when studying the Media in English.

MEDIA AND TECHNOLOGY: THE PRACTICAL DIMENSION

One of the distinctive and attractive features of studying the Media has been the opportunity to get to grips with technology and make our own media texts; we do our learners a grave disservice if we do not enable them to take charge of some of these media, so that they can understand how they can be creators of media texts as well as consumers and analysers of them.

We live in fortunate times, as developments in readily available technology mean that we can all, for example:

- design and print quality documents using word processors and desktop publishing software
- design and upload websites
- edit and produce digital video films
- create television programmes
- broadcast our own radio station on the Internet
- record and edit digital sound
- create animations using computer software.

Indeed, the practical part of Media Studies has always been an attractive aspect of the subject when learners have chosen it at GCSE or A level. Also, it is worth pointing out here that boys in particular can be motivated to apply themselves in Media Studies – it is the powerful mix of practical application, possibly involving aspects of ICT, and the exploration of seemingly familiar texts (for example, soap opera, pop music videos, advertisements) that seems to make the subject very accessible for them. In addition, we should not underestimate the teaching and learning advantages of harmonizing in one subject area the three main learning styles, namely, visual, auditory, and kinaesthetic.

So far, then, we have established that Media Studies as part of English has the potential to:

- develop the notion of 'text' into a broader conceptualization
- bring a significantly different practical element to English
- introduce a set of concepts that are intellectually rigorous and educationally valid
- broaden learners' understanding of the subject into aspects of cultural analysis

- acknowledge the expertise about their culture that the learners bring to the classroom
- enable a range of assessment devices to be used to provide valid feedback on the distinctive learning opportunities in studying the Media.

Connecting literary and media texts

(a) How might you go about enabling learners to understand that a literary text is as much the product of choices – about sequencing of events, about setting, about names of characters – as a film or television programme?

(b) How could you enable them to see a literary text as a 'product' to be marketed, advertised, and sold?

Clues

For (a), you might want to seek out examples of the drafts of texts written in the process of making the final version. You could also make good connections with the processes the learners go through in their own writing.

You could also give learners texts that have been cut up into sections, and ask them to re-create the text, providing reasons for their decisions. That way they see how narrative sequencing is done.

For (b), you will need to collect material associated with a recent bestseller – bookshops and publishers can be very helpful. Looking at how bookshops market books – window displays, special offers, book signings – and how customers are made aware of books – product placement, special displays, use of book jackets.

That could lead to designing plans to publicize an existing book so as to make it a bestseller.

PLANNING FOR TEACHING AND LEARNING WHEN STUDYING THE MEDIA

What follows is a collection of possible activities that might form part of a Unit of Study on 'Soap Opera'. The intention is that later you will return to this list and make selections as appropriate.

Soap Opera has been chosen as the main textual resource because:

- the vast majority of teenagers watch at least one
- it is a popular television genre with both teenagers and adults

- soap operas regularly hit the headlines, over content or new characters
- there is a rich variety of products that at the same time share a number of distinguishing features.

And now the list.

- Make a list of all the current television soap operas.
- Plot the viewing times of all the soaps.
- In a typical episode, count the number of:
  - characters seen
  - storylines encountered
  - locations used.
- Try drawing a map of the locality.
- Visually represent the relationship connections between the characters met.
- What are the distinguishing features of soap opera?
- Why are some serials not soap operas? (*The Bill* v. *EastEnders*)?
- How are particular groups of characters represented – women, teenagers, black people?
- What different audiences do soaps cater for? How do we know?
- Can you find information on viewing figures for soaps?
- Which soaps are most popular with your age group? How could you find out?
- Why are soap operas so named?
- If you were proposing a new soap opera, where would you set it?
- What other aspects of your proposed soap do you think you should present to a commissioning editor?
- Try writing an episode for an existing soap, or the opening episode from your proposed new one.
- Try planning a week's worth of broadcasts for a soap in terms of storylines.

Here, then, we have yet another example of how a holistic approach to learning in English can provide fertile combinations of elements, offering learners and teachers alike a freshness of perspective that can only be to the benefit of all.

It is now time to return to the earlier mind map of activities using soap operas.

Your task is to design a Unit of Study, using proformas and templates in the appendices, for a Key Stage 3 class, on Soap Opera that contains:

- clear learning objectives, matched to appropriate National Curriculum ATs
- an outline sequence of lessons, leading to clearly defined outcomes (in terms of products)
- a choice of activities from the list appropriately applied for learners to learn specific aspects at specific stages of the Unit
- additional tasks created as appropriate, especially where none of the above fit your particular learning purpose(s)
- evidence that you have considered the questions:
  - How will I know that the learners have achieved my learning objectives?
  - What evidence will I need to collect?
  - How will I assess any oral contributions?
  - How will I keep on-going records as well as final grades/marks?

Soap Opera may not appeal to you. If so, generate your own mind map of activities around a particular aspect or feature of a medium (for example, radio, or music videos), and then design a Unit of Study using the same prompt questions as in Activity 8.2.

MEDIA IN ENGLISH AND ASSESSMENT

There still remains for some people the vexed question of assessment; it is an integral part of the critique of Media Studies in some quarters that, just as the definition of the subject is vague, so any assessment of products and processes is subject to the same vagueness. Given the arguments presented so far, it will not surprise you that there are answers to that criticism as well.

In the British Film Institute's *Secondary Media Education: A Curriculum Statement* (BFI, 1991), there is a section on 'Assessment principles for media learning'. The heading is significant, in that the authors could have entitled it 'Principles for assessing media', whereas they connect 'assessment' and 'learning' very closely, as they should be, a point to be developed a little later. But first, the principles:

1. Demonstration and application of key areas of knowledge and understanding – connections to the previously described six key areas (Agencies: who is communicating and why? Categories: what kind of text is it? Technologies: how is it produced? Languages: how do we know what it means? Audiences: who receives it, and what sense do they make of it? Representations: how does it present its subject(s)?).

2. The acquisition of specialist language – the use of semantically correct terminology.

3. Formalized reflection – analysis, observation, description, comparison.

4. Social and organizational skills – practical, collaborative.

5. Production skills – use of a range of Media technology (BFI, 1991: 98–9).

The attempt here is to value and validate the distinctive features of studying the Media in the assessment process. It would make an interesting short activity to take the five principles above and connect them to what has been said already about teaching and learning in Media Education.

Notice in particular how close the links are between what is to be learned and the assessment criteria, again suggestive of implementation of current understandings of good practice – a teacher's learning objectives are, of necessity, her/his assessment criteria.

Some mentions have been made of assessment in Media. In a sense, studying the Media in English provides a range of assessment opportunities for the Attainment Targets in English: Speaking and Listening, Reading, and Writing. And that is highly appropriate, as can be seen from the references to the assessment of Speaking and Listening in Activity 8.2 above.

However, this chapter has also argued for a distinctive set of learning opportunities when studying the Media, so it would be logical to expect a distinctive set of assessment emphases to emerge at the same time. The *processes* of assessment may be very similar whether the teacher is assessing aspects of the Attainment Targets or distinctively Media aspects.

However, the *focus* for assessment may well have distinctive Media aspects to it. Or both may be happening at the same time. So it would be a useful exercise to return to any Unit of Study you have devised in response to previous tasks, and add to it very specific assessment opportunities. You will need to be very clear about **what** you are assessing and **how** you are to assess it. Try to put into practice what is recommended in this chapter by using the British Film Institute's five assessment criteria from the *Curriculum Statement* (BFI, 1991) as a framework for ensuring that the assessment strategies do justice to the distinctiveness of media products and processes. To that end, it will be important to achieve an appropriate balance between the assessment of processes and the assessment of outcomes.

CONCLUSION

There is still something particularly exciting about studying with learners aspects of Media. Part of that excitement is the frisson of working with learners very much on their cultural terms, and there can be real benefits in passing the mantle of the expert over to them for once.

Also, the practical components of Media study are an innovation for most learners in English, especially if you have the equipment and the confidence to use some technologically advanced equipment – for example, digital video and still cameras, computer hardware and software, sound sampling, recoding and editing equipment.

In other words, English seen through media perspectives takes on quite a different appearance, and one that may well appeal to learners differently from the 'normal' English lesson. At the same time, we can argue strongly for maintaining a holistic view of English, as defined by the ATs, while focusing on distinctive features of a particular aspect of the subject.

KEY TEXTS

The Film Education website (currently at www.filmeducation.org) is well worth a visit. Many of the resources and approaches are adaptable to additional media.

The English and Media Centre (currently at www.englishandmedia.co.uk) produces a wealth of resources for teaching pupils and a range of stimulating books to inspire teachers. Of particular note are *The Key Stage 3 Media Book* and *The Key Stage 4 Media Pack*.

CHAPTER NINE

ICT in English

KEY FEATURES OF THE AREA OF STUDY

INTRODUCTION

Today we can reflect that the educational applications of Information and Communication Technology (ICT) have been through very significant changes. For those of us in the field of secondary English, the movement from Information Technology (IT) to ICT has been very important, signalling as it does the progress towards using the technology for communications. And that is where English teachers ought to get excited.

ICT was, in the first place, the domain of the computer expert. The main curriculum consequences of that were:

- a separation of ICT from other subjects
- the teaching of computer programming.

Alongside those developments in the introduction of ICT into the curriculum was a fervent hope in some quarters that ICT would eventually dominate the learning experience – the vision was individual learners in front of computer screens where resources and tests would be provided by the software and be quite separate from the teacher. Indeed, there were some who predicted the end of the teacher, as so called 'programmed learning' would make teachers redundant.

We may find such views laughable now, but we should remember where we have come from and where we are now in terms of using computers for learning and teaching. There has been progress, but some vestiges of the 'old thinking' still remain; we need to be alert to such views, as it is important that we develop a set of principles to inform how we make best use of the exciting technological developments of recent years.

At this moment, it is important to state that as English/Literacy teachers our aim is not to teach ICT in English. On the contrary, the stance offered here is that using ICT in English provides:

- resources for learning, in terms of access to distinctive types of texts
- distinctive processes for learning, especially in terms of creating digital texts
- unrivalled and easily accessible ways of communicating visually, orally and in writing.

ICT serves to enhance the subject, to support learning in Speaking and Listening, Reading, and Writing, at word, sentence and text levels. We cannot ignore technological developments, but we can make sure we adapt and apply them to the purpose of teaching pupils about the literacy demands and opportunities of the present and future.

There is one more important point that must be made: ICT is not solely about computers. In much of what follows, it will read as though ICT equals computers, mainly because many of the challenging developments have been with computers. However, we must not ignore the potential for communication of many other pieces of technology: digital cameras, fax machines, overhead projectors, television and video, radio, tape recorders, to name but a few.

Many of us can remember using technology in English lessons when we were pupils/students, and English teachers have a noble tradition of seeking out the learning potential of new inventions.

PAUSE

Try to remember a lesson (in school/college, in higher education) that involved the use of some technology (*not* a computer). What differences did the technology make to your participation in the lesson?

Recent technological developments have dramatically altered our view of what it is to communicate with others. For example, we now regularly:

- write more emails than we ever wrote letters
- send faxes from our desktop computers
- send information via the internet (e.g., each time we buy a book or CD online)
- send documents, pictures, sound files as email attachments to family, friends and colleagues
- write at a computer screen in preference to pen and paper
- rely on digital technology and software for diary, address book, birthday reminders, to do lists
- use a mobile phone to send text messages as well as speak to people
- prefer an interactive whiteboard in the classroom rather than chalk or marker pen.

PAUSE

Which items of communication technology do you regularly use? Make your own list.

We cannot put the genie back in the bottle. What we can do is apply the technology in a principled way for the benefit of our pupils' learning and progress in English. In other words, let us use the potential of the technology to enhance the communications our pupils make, so that they see the processes and products of communication as essential facets of being literate.

These are exciting times. Processes once thought of as beyond the scope of most of us, such as animation and digital video editing, are becoming much more accessible in terms of cost and ease of use. We can demystify Disney and the BBC in our classrooms, for the benefit of our pupils.

For teachers, there are the challenges and the opportunities for using new technology in the pedagogic processes. We are, for example, only beginning to understand the impact of interactive whiteboards on our pupils' learning and on teachers' perceptions of teaching – are there distinctive features of good practice to identify and theorize?

At the same time, there are still pressures to use programmed learning, despite knowing that the learning gains of such programs and processes do not appear to be long lasting or transferable to other contexts. We knew that about spelling tests, so why do we expect programmed learning to be any different? But that debate is for another time! At this stage, it is enough to say that there are better uses for hardware and software than programmed learning. We can be certain of that, because we are setting processes and purposes for communication at the heart of what we do with ICT in English – there is still much to recommend the active consideration of audience and purpose whenever planning for learning in English happens.

ICT AND ENGLISH: PRINCIPLES

The Cox Report, the forerunner of the first version of English in the National Curriculum, has a very helpful phrase; it mentions that: 'Pupils should continue to develop in their dual roles as *makers of meanings in their own texts* and as *receivers and makers of meaning in the texts of others.*' [Emphases added] (DES, 1989: paragraph 17.22) Communication is a two-way process involving what we want to communicate and what others want to communicate to us. Communication is also about how we process what others communicate to us, as well as how we make accessible what we are trying to communicate to others. It is, therefore, about the choices communicators make:

- We all know what a difference one word can make ('I really like/love you').
- Do we choose simple sentences for young readers?
- Stories sometimes carry more powerful meanings than other kinds of texts.

Choices at word, sentence and text levels have been deliberately chosen because recent developments in the teaching of literacy (the National Literacy Strategy) have highlighted those three aspects as effective ways of exploring language so that learners can develop their own communication skills.

Developments in ICT have added significantly to the list of kinds of texts we can now create. And some of those texts can only be created using ICT. We therefore have the potential to add to the list of text types that pupils can ultimately choose from in their quest to communicate effectively and powerfully.

For example:

- Combining words with pictures and sounds – a multimedia text – and then displaying the text on a screen can be done digitally.

- A website presents unique opportunities to communicate with the world through the creation of a distinctive type of text that requires distinctive textual and technological skills to create it.

In other words, ICT presents English with the possibility of connecting its core principles with opportunities created by the new technology, thus enhancing the subject while remaining true to what we hold dear. We see that the technology adds to the types of texts we can create as well as read – we can 'write' such texts as well as 'consume' them.

ICT AND ENGLISH: DISTINCTIVE FEATURES

It is time to develop the notion of the distinctiveness of the contribution of ICT to English. An important principle here is that we ought to be exploring how ICT enables distinctive learning to take place, so that learners are aware of the special contribution of ICT to literacy learning and progress.

For example, with an electronic dictionary it is possible to search for all words that originate from a particular language. It would be very time-consuming to do the same thing with a paper dictionary. Such an activity presents a unique opportunity to explore a feature of English, in this case its incorporation of words from a variety of other languages.

But before there is any further exploration of distinctive processes, we need to acknowledge the existence of the 'electronic text'. When text is loaded into a word processor, it becomes electronically malleable in a number of distinctive ways:

- It can be 'exploded', so that lists of words and their frequency can be examined.
- You can search and replace words and/or phrases, sometimes with humorous intent, but also for serious exploration of, say, the linguistic implications of doing a gender swap on a story.
- New text can be inserted, blocks of existing text can be rearranged.

All the time that a text is being manipulated in such ways, it remains 'neat and tidy' on the screen, still maintaining its appearance of a 'proper' piece of writing.

Some of the digital texts we read require particular reading skills; coping with teletext or an 'information rich' Internet home page, for example, places emphasis on skimming and scanning skills, while texts that combine images with words can pose complex reading strategies.

Those skills are acquired in other, earlier contexts; most of us, for example, learned to deal with words and pictures in the early days of our reading development with picturebooks, proceeded to reading comics, and then as adults some of us like graphical novels – comic books for grown-ups. However, it is helpful to think of aspects of literacy that are emphasized by the digital revolution, and so the concept of e-literacy was born.

PAUSE

What other aspects of e-literacy can you identify? It may help to consider:

- the style of writing you use for emails – do you use letter style, or some other?
- the language of text messages, Internet chat rooms, etc.

ICT AND ENGLISH: DISTINCTIVE PROCESSES

As well as the distinctiveness of the texts we can read and create with ICT, there are some aspects of ICT in English we need to know about, as they have an impact on both the planning for learning and the management of learning. Some brief examples will help make the relevant points:

- Computer monitor screens make writing potentially very visible to lots of people. What are the implications of that for working on, say, personal writing in a computer room with lots of workstations? Does collaborative writing around the monitor screen work effectively?
- If there are two or three computers in your normal classroom, how are you going to plan for their use in a lesson?
- With all the care in the world, it is still possible to stumble into inappropriate websites. What rules would you want to be in operation for such eventualities?
- Computers provide wonderful facilities for capturing the various stages of the writing process. How would you plan to save each version of, say, a story, and how might you use the intermediate versions of the text with pupils?

- In what ways can we think of ICT as providing a practical element for English? Does the possibility of real readers and real audiences 'out there' make a significant difference for our pupils? If so, how do we exploit safely the advantages of email, collaborative writing across the world, chat rooms, video conferencing, school websites – to name but a few possibilities?

There are clear implications for resources (hardware and software), and for their location (in classrooms, in dedicated computer suites). There are also implications for systematic planning for ICT opportunities in English in units of study as well as in individual lessons. Just like all the other kinds of texts we meet in English lessons, and the attendant processes of 'dealing with them', so we need to think of ICT in English as providing distinctive resources and processes for learning in English.

OPPORTUNITIES FOR DISTINCTIVE LEARNING

First, an activity. So far, we have made big assumptions about your personal competence with ICT. Now you need to be honest, and start planning for developments in three areas:

- your personal competence and confidence with the hardware and software
- your ability to use ICT for professional purposes
- your ability to use ICT with pupils in the classroom.

One way of doing that is to audit existing knowledge, understanding and skills. The process will have clear implications for your future learning and development. The questions that follow are designed to enable you to comply with the relevant requirements for becoming a qualified teacher and are framed in the context of currently applicable Standards for Qualified Teacher Status (QTS).

Auditing ICT

Personal competence
- Are you content with your ability to use a word processor, a database, a spreadsheet, presentation software (e.g., Microsoft's PowerPoint)?
- Can you use email to send messages, to send attachments?

- Can you use an Internet search engine effectively?
- Are you able to create multimedia texts (combining words, pictures, sounds)?
- Do you know how to use hyperlinks in, for example, a word processor file, on a web page, in PowerPoint?
- Can you manipulate picture files, using appropriate software?

Using ICT for professional purposes
- Can you design a worksheet using a word processor? Can you justify your uses of colour, font (size and style), and layout?
- How can you use a database to monitor pupils' progress?
- How can a spreadsheet provide you with useful information from numerical data?
- What possibilities does an English Department website provide for you, your colleagues and your pupils?

Using ICT with pupils
- What classroom management and lesson planning issues does using the computer suite/the three computers at the back of your classroom pose for you?
- What kinds of activities make best and distinctive use of the hardware and software?
- How can you plan for the use of ICT during processes, e.g., in the writing process, in the preparation of a group presentation?
- Argue from experience for the advantages of using a computer generated simulation with pupils in English.
- What safety rules would you advocate when pupils are dealing with email and the Internet? Have you found any examples of good whole-school policies?

Do not expect to answer all the questions at the first read through. But by the end of the course, you should be able to provide evidence for having addressed each one. So it is a good idea to:

- Set targets (e.g., learn to use a word processor [WP]).

- Set success criteria (e.g., produce a worksheet using a WP; require pupils to create a piece of writing with hotlinks in it using a WP).

- Keep evidence of the processes of your learning (e.g., the address of a helpful website that introduced you to a number of interesting and applicable features of a WP).

- Keep evidence of the outcomes of your learning (e.g., the first ever WP worksheet, a more recent one with commentary on developments; a lesson plan where ICT is an important element).

- Celebrate achievements.

PLANNING FOR LEARNING USING ATTAINMENT TARGETS

ICT AND SPEAKING AND LISTENING

- Tasks that require pupils to solve problems that involve a computer can generate a lot of 'process talk' around the screen (e.g., making decisions about the design of a homepage for the school's online prospectus).

- Computer generated simulations that rely on a stream of data require pupils to organize themselves and the data, and thus generate a rich variety of talk, often in realistically pressurized situations (e.g., the Newsroom Simulation, about which more later).

- Pupils will have to consider speaking and listening issues when doing a presentation (singly, in groups) with presentation software (e.g., Microsoft's PowerPoint), and be able to reflect on the effectiveness of their own and others' presentations.

ICT AND READING

- We need to expose pupils to the range of digital texts they can encounter via the Internet, CD-ROM, e-books.

- We can explore with pupils the range of reading skills needed to cope with the distinctive reading demands of digital texts.

- We should define and describe the features of those digital texts that have no paper-based equivalent, especially those that are non-linear, multi-layered (e.g., web pages with hyperlinks) and that offer the reader choices in the course of which the reader 'creates' her/his own text (e.g., branching stories, information on CD-ROM).

- Word processors offer us opportunities to explore easily the effects on the reader of changing font style, introducing colour, changing font size, changing layout.

- Word processors enable us to read for particular purposes, so that we can, for example, highlight adjectives, change the colour of the key word in each sentence, alter the sequence of paragraphs.

ICT AND WRITING

- Much has been made already in this chapter of the possibilities for creating distinctive texts using ICT.

- We need to explore and develop the implications for the writing process when using a word processor, so that we are aware of ways of using a WP to advantage at various stages of writing (e.g., keeping records of mind maps in the early stages of preparation; using paragraph headings to give shape to the text, and then filling in the gaps; creating a text in a non-linear way, so that conclusions are written before the argument is developed; making notes during writing, so that ideas that suddenly emerge are not lost).

- Pupils need to know how to make discriminatory and critical use of particular features of word processors, e.g., copy and paste, spell checkers and grammar checkers, layout choices, style choices (especially in desktop publishing software).

- The implications of writing for real audiences, e.g., younger pupils.

- Using email for collaborative writing.

- Publishing work on the Internet, giving and receiving reviews.

ICT in English must aim to offer a distinctive and special experience. Sometimes, some things are best done on paper with a pen. But there are some things that can only be done in English with ICT, and we ought to seek out those opportunities. Just as our colleagues in the past used tape recorders so memorably in English lessons, so, whenever there is a new technological development in the world of ICT, we should think: how can I use that in English? At the time of writing, digital video editing (DVE) is becoming much more available in schools:

- Digital video camera prices are coming down.

- Hardware and software for computers are readily available at reasonable prices.

- The processor speeds and storage capacities of modern personal computers mean that it is now feasible to manipulate large amounts of data very effectively.

Why should English teachers be getting excited about DVE? If we apply the principles already mentioned, we see that:

- DVE enables pupils to have control of a very powerful medium, the moving image, and to be able to use it for purposes that they define, so becoming producers as well as critical consumers
- moving image texts created with DVE can be made available to viewers via the Internet
- working with DVE not only requires the technical know-how, but also understanding about narrative sequencing, genre, audience and purpose
- DVE makes the creation of moving image texts available to all.

We want our pupils to be 'makers of meaning', as producers as well as consumers, we want all to have equal access to the means of communication, and we want pupils to be able to realize in their own products their own purposes for wanting to communicate – and to be able to rationalize and reflect on their choices.

WHAT IT CAN LOOK LIKE IN PRACTICE

In this part of the chapter, there are *three* aims:

- to provide some prompt questions to guide your observations of ICT in English in schools
- to present a sample Unit of Study for using ICT in English
- to set you thinking about applying the principles and practices presented so far.

OBSERVING ICT IN ENGLISH

I hope the following questions and suggestions prove useful in identifying good practices in the uses of ICT in English:

- Whenever ICT is used in English, be on the alert for the distinctive/special/unique elements provided by ICT.

- ICT in English is at its best when the ICT is so well integrated into the learning activities that the boundaries between ICT and the rest of English are hardly to be seen.
- What range of software is being used?
- Are some of the distinctive features of the software being used to advantage for pupils' learning in English?
- What rules are in operation when ICT is used?
- What implications for the overall management of the classroom, the pupils, and resources are there?
- Is there a balance of learning styles in the activities required of the pupils, so that there is group/pair work as well as individual work?
- What judgements can you make about the effectiveness of the learning?
- What connections can you see between the choice of activities, the aspects of English that the pupils are learning, and the uses of ICT?

A SAMPLE UNIT OF STUDY FOR USING ICT IN ENGLISH

The unit that follows is based on experience of working with trainee teachers and school pupils using software that generates a simulation. We have tried not to be too idealistic, but please remember that we are not suggesting you try to replicate this exactly. What we are presenting is an example that worked in particular sets of circumstances. Any ideas you wish to use from this example will have to be adapted to the context you are in.

Unit Title: Newsroom Simulation: Radio News
Class
Year 10
Time
First Unit, Spring Term
Learning objectives
By the end of this unit, pupils will:

- **know about**
    - the variety of ways news is presented on the radio
    - about the varieties of talk necessary for the task
    - about the functions of writing and reading in such a task.

- **understand about**

    – roles in a group

    – individually how they contributed to the group

    – the need for variety in talk (questioning, supporting, performing)

    – audience and purpose in the media.

- **be able to**

    – work to tight deadlines

    – work co-operatively in a group

    – define a role/contribution within the group

    – contribute particular literacy skills to the task.

Sequence of activities

Preparation

(i) Analysing radio news (taped examples): types of bulletin, length, number of stories, lead stories, end stories, variety of styles by station.

(ii) The world of the newsroom (possible use of film examples), roles in newsroom group.

(iii) Importance of deadlines.

(iv) Designing a new radio station – notions of audience, purpose, market research. (What do people listen to on the radio? What might people like to listen to that is not currently provided?)

Implementation

(i)   Planning for roles.
(ii)   Defining the task.
(iii) Running the computer-generated simulation.
(iv)   Presenting the products.

Reflection

(i)   Defining the learning.
(ii)   'If I did this again, I would … '.
(iii) Evaluating outcomes against agreed criteria.
(iv)   Writing up the learning in terms of the process as well as the product.

ICT opportunities

(i)   The newsroom simulation.

(ii) Use of teletext, the Web for up to date news stories during the running of the simulation (to add authenticity).

(iii) Use of WP for newsreader's script.

(iv) Use of WP to copy and paste news from the Web into script.

(v)   Use of computer monitor as teleprompter for reading of news.

(vi) Use of tape recorder for 'vox pop' effect.

Assessment opportunities

(i)   Monitoring of pupil achievements/strengths during the simulation via page-a-pupil book.

(ii) Products assessed against a set of criteria agreed with the group.

(iii) Pupil self-evaluation using sheet provided, to include targets for next time.

(iv) Pupils' diary writing during lessons.

(v)   Reflective writing: 'The development of my speaking and listening skills'.

(vi) The Chief Radio News Editor's report on the effectiveness of the radio newsroom team (imaginative writing based on diary observations).

Learning outcomes

(i)   A two-minute radio news bulletin performed by each group.

(ii) Writing from individuals.

(iii) Group presentations with documents for new radio station.

Additional comments

The simulation at the heart of the Unit delivers to the groups acting as newsrooms in a range of different radio stations a stream of information about a breaking story. In addition, the groups have access to the day's news via the daily newspapers and, if available, teletext and web-based news services.

By a given time, each group must prepare and rehearse for performance a two-minute radio news bulletin that is appropriate in style and content for the station type chosen and created.

Each group will get a printout from the computer of the piece of news. One person from each group will act as 'runner' to collect the news and make sure that everyone in the group is aware of the latest development. Groups will be encouraged to assign roles in the group, such as editor, reader, reporter, writer, librarian – someone to manage the mass of paper.

The simulation effectively 'runs the lesson', in that the constant interruptions of the printer become the focal point of the lesson as the groups battle to cope with the demands of the quantity of news and the pressure of the deadline.

The teacher is very effectively released to do other things:

• observe group dynamics

• make notes on the range of talk types used during the simulation

• monitor individual pupils

• make assessments of individuals against explicit criteria.

APPLYING THE PRINCIPLES AND PRACTICES PRESENTED SO FAR

The example above focuses very much on aspects of Speaking and Listening in the context of gathering evidence on which to make a judgement for a summative grade for the GCSE examination in English. In thinking about designing your own unit of study, you will, of course, have to pay due attention to the context of your school experience. Nevertheless, we hope you find the example above at least a workable template for whatever you have or choose to do with ICT in English.

It is still true to say that much of what happens with ICT in secondary English is innovative, so there are plenty of ways to be exciting and different. If thinking about using ICT in English does anything, it ought to make each of us return to the fundamental principles that continue to inform the best practices in classrooms with pupils. So, how can using ICT enable more pupils to write with greater confidence and greater readiness than before? While the skills of sustained writing are not to be underestimated, at the same time we ought to be encouraging pupils to make choices from the range of e-texts that it is now possible to create. The day is not far off when the skills required to create a website will not be given the minority status they currently enjoy. And we have not begun to consider the likely impact of speech recognition software, software that changes sounds into letters on the screen.

CONCLUSION

These are truly exciting times for teaching and learning in English. At last we are beginning to see a more consistent application of a core of pedagogic principles associated with the subject – and we are starting to see the positive effects and gains for our pupils.

But there is much yet to do, and the application of principles in practice is as yet far too patchy. The people who read this chapter are the people most likely to make a difference in the uses of ICT in English, because they are either aware of how much they need to know, or they understand the importance of facing and applying the challenge of the new. I hope this chapter has contributed to your feeling that whatever your starting point, the task ahead of you is eminently achievable – and might turn out to be fun along the way.

KEY TEXTS

Goodwyn, A. (ed.) (2000) *English in the Digital Age*. London: Cassell.

Leask, M. and Pachler, N. (1999) *Learning to Teach Using ICT in the Secondary School*. London: Routledge.

Snyder, I. (ed.) (1998) *Page to Screen: Taking Literacy into the Electronic Era*. London: Routledge.

There are a number of government ICT initiatives on the Internet. You may want to explore the resources and articles on the NGfL website (www.ngfl.gov.uk) and the BECTA website (www.becta.org.uk).

CHAPTER TEN

The Future of English

> developments ... are directing attention away from the page to the screen, from the pen to the mouse and from a well-structured essay to a well-organised Web site.
>
> (Millard, 2000: 181)

In this chapter we will try to anticipate some of the future trends you will be witness to in the early years of your career as an English teacher. This is a high-risk and, possibly, foolhardy activity, given the number of political moves on the English curriculum chessboard. But the dynamic of national interest is accompanied by global trends that are likely to be equally powerful agents for shaping the future of English teaching. This makes for an exciting cultural experience!

ICT CHANGES LITERACY

There is no doubting the significance of these two iconic terms in the futures of English teaching, as ICT prises open the traditional notions of what it means to be literate. National governments are investing heavily in both agendas – in ways that seem often to point in opposite directions. The National Grid for Learning and the British Educational Communication and Technology Agency (BECTA) exist to take the electronic revolution to every classroom and staffroom, so that the screen is at least as important a pedagogic tool as the page. Meanwhile, the KS3 Strategy in the secondary English classroom often seems to promote an older model of print-based learning and testing.

But first let us consider the future impact of ICT on the careers of current trainee English teachers. You will belong to the first generation of teachers for whom the written, linear text will be one literacy amongst others, and, perhaps more crucially, you will be teaching generations who have absorbed the potential of electronic literacies from their earliest moments.

Mackey (2002), in a fascinating ethnography of sixteen young readers between the ages of 10 and 14, explores the new boundaries of literacy for those growing up with commercial and technological fictions such *Harry Potter, Lord of the Rings* and *The Simpsons*. She chooses the label of 'extreme literacies' to describe the multimedia options that accompany these global 'events' – from computer games, to print 'fanzines', from websites carrying reviews, film scripts, news bulletins and chat rooms to the primary written fiction itself. Whilst the fashionable moment for each 'story' might come and go, these patterns of literacy will become more and more established.

For English teachers, multimedia technology offers a textual universe that has to be explored to ensure that we are preparing learners to enjoy a full contemporary literacy. You will have to support young 'readers' of the Internet in selecting from the bombardment of textual possibilities; for yourself, you might need to re-conceptualize the reading process to engage in non-linear, simultaneous, split-screen or pathway literacies. The classroom of the future will invite young people to become active producers of computer-generated texts, with an instant global audience and potential control over the whole production process – arguably a very brave new world if compared to the captive consumers of the published text sitting in many of our contemporary 'unwired' English classrooms.

Whilst access to computers does nothing in itself to promote greater equality of educational opportunity for pupils (see Snyder, Angus and Sutherland-Smith, 2002, for an Australian slant on this issue), English teachers of the future will need to be significant stakeholders in a school's ICT investment if the subject is going to remain central to the multiple literacy needs and interests of generations of young people. The English teacher will need to be an enthusiastic proponent of multimedia literacy, rather than the stubborn defender of a print-based culture that served earlier generations. As Mary Hilton has suggested, 'the new illiterates are people who can use only one communication technology' (Hilton, 2003: 61); English teachers must not allow themselves or their pupils to join the ranks of the electronically dispossessed.

And how will government-promoted models of literacy fare in this brave new world? Whilst moving-image media and ICT-based information texts are statutory elements of National Curriculum English, the Framework provides only a nod in this direction (of some ninety-eight objectives for Year 7 English, only three refer explicitly to multimedia technology). 'Framework' literacy is hemmed in by objectives, targets and testing, and you will need a clear head to formulate a dynamic literacy curriculum that layers pupils' personal digital enthusiasms and expertise onto the officially sanctioned literacy programmes found in the Key Stage 3 Strategy. We would predict that trainee English teachers over the next few years will be pioneers in settling this newly named territory, if literacy in the secondary school is to become an expansive and progressive movement.

WHAT'S IN A NAME? ENGLISH OR CULTURAL STUDIES

English will become an increasingly plural idea/concept. Perhaps the second global trend to affect English teachers at the start of the twenty-first century is the changing role of the English language in world markets. Whilst you might think this concerns English as a foreign language (EFL) teachers, the impact will be felt in native British classrooms of the future, as population movements and Internet communications make for both greater local diversity and more international standardization of English. These issues were touched on in Chapter 2 and the intention here is only to signal the possible relocation of secondary English at these cultural crossroads. Andrews (2001) comments on the inadequacy of the term 'English' to grasp the essence of the subject in the new digital communication universe. Pupils in native UK classrooms will increasingly belong to multiple speech communities based not only in the home, but in global chat rooms and Internet cafés. Language becomes a lifestyle commodity, a mark of local identity and an international status-symbol, and these trends will shape the English language in ways that English teachers must continue to track.

Graddol (2001) has suggested that Britain's monolingualism may become a cultural and economic liability in future years, as the dominance of English as the Internet language recedes and varieties of English far-removed from native UK English become global realities. In this scenario, English teachers in UK classrooms will need to act as cultural ambassadors to ensure that their pupils can participate confidently in this global language marketplace. In this international trading, those voices clamouring for special protection for the literary heritage sound decidedly dated. English teachers of the future should properly be concerned to locate English literature within world literature and to link local language variety to global trends, if they are to support their pupils as world citizens.

THE TESTING CULTURE

Whilst engaging with these powerful global movements, English teachers will need to be listening to the voices of national government(s). It is likely that government voices will grow louder and more strident, as world trends continue to threaten their power bases. Currently, and probably persistently into the near future, governments will make most noise about assessment and testing. Arguably, national testing in England has become a centralized control mechanism to keep at bay the dynamic global forces hinted at earlier.

Consider the battery of assessment issues which have crowded the national educational agenda from 2000 to 2002: optional tests for Years 7 and 8; booster materials for Year 9; changes to KS3 tests and mark schemes; AS and A2 developments and crisis over grading; vocational qualifications within a revised 14–19 assessment framework. Viewed through an international lens, this paper empire looks faintly ridiculous and certainly parochial. Instead, on-line testing could provide a highly flexible, individually tailored assessment system allowing teachers to apply tests at the point of need and to use assessment information diagnostically; and teachers could be preparing global citizens of the future for internationally recognized examinations that provide educational passports to global job markets.

Beginning professionals will have to decide how to respond to this agenda, and English teachers have, in the recent past, been significant shapers of this agenda. The National Association for the Teaching of English (NATE), which has provided a sustained professional counterpoint to government voices, has recently spoken up against 'objectives-led teaching' – the main pedagogical thrust in the KS3 Strategy (Wrigley, 2003). In an attempt to reposition English for the future, Wrigley reminds English teachers of the continuing importance of 'subjectives-led learning'. Newly qualified teachers will have to make their own accommodations here, but the challenge is clearly to ensure that individual learner needs are not replaced by year group targets and percentage scores, whatever government and school pressures appear to demand.

One such accommodation will take place around the kind of assessment you want to use to support teaching. Will word- and sentence-level analysis take over from text-level teaching? Will tests assess learners' achievements fairly? Will national mark schemes continue to emphasize 'correctness' and technical skills over content and voice? The devil is in the detail, and beginning English teachers will need to work hard to ensure the holistic principles of assessment are not eroded by the testing culture (see D'Arcy, 2000, for an interesting critique of government models of assessment). They will need, in particular, to appreciate how the detail fits into the bigger picture and to do their best to sustain a broader perspective on assessment than that provided through national testing. Wiliam and Black

(1998; 2002) find that teachers' professional practices are what get the results, not the number of tests pupils do. Their influential research is showing that formative assessment, peer assessment and the quality of teacher–pupil classroom interaction are crucial factors in improving pupil learning.[1] This suggests a liberating course for beginner teachers, supported by subject associations like NATE, but one that steers away from government policy, as it currently stands.

INCLUSION OR EXCLUSION?

Education policy-makers in the UK might find they have internal contradictions of their own to resolve at the beginning of the twenty-first century. Whilst testing and assessment is one major strand of policy, so too is inclusion, and the two together do not make a satisfactory weave. Inclusion is a declared theme in each subject component of NC English, requiring teachers to 'respond to pupils' diverse learning needs' and to 'overcome potential barriers to learning for individuals and groups of pupils'. This theme was subsequently underpinned by a substantial resource bank to promote awareness of EAL learners' needs (DfES, 2002d; TTA, 2000).

There is, however, much professional concern that the government's testing regime is pushing more and more pupils to the margins, at the very moment when government is funding schools to address individual need. Government targets for pupil achievement at KS3 require increasing numbers of pupils to reach 'the average Level 5' (currently 75 per cent to reach Level 5 in English by 2004 and 85 per cent by 2007). This levering up of expectation is not based on predictions about pupils' current achievement but on government electoral priorities. What happens to the notion of the average in this context? Can teachers embrace the principle of inclusion, with its painstaking attention to the needs of the individual, whilst keeping an eye on such demanding national targets? And what happens to the 15 per cent or 25 per cent who sit outside the government project?

Professional teachers and researchers have begun to identify some of the losers: native UK children whose language and/or cultural backgrounds do not fit neatly with the standard English expectations of the NLS and NC English (Kearney, 2000; King, 2002); SEN pupils (Smith and Hardman, 2000) and more broadly, those pupils whose patterns of learning and social maturity require more space and time than the highly focused interaction of the NLS allows (Allen, 2002). In the coming years, teachers will need a keen eye to sift professional from political imperatives, if they are to meet the needs of their pupils in ways that are both manageable and professionally satisfying. We sincerely believe that Wrigley's stark description of the recent educational scene can be transformed by teachers working collectively to reclaim their professional turf:

> The unusually high status given to standardized national testing and the increasingly single-minded emphasis on interventions and booster classes while clustered under the banners of entitlement and inclusion, are actually becoming a kind of linguistic imperialism which pays insufficient regard to current and local language usage.
>
> **(Wrigley, 2003: 1)**

TEXT AS THE COMPASS

Throughout this book we have held to the notion of *text(s)* as the central motif of English teaching in the future. The study of texts, in their infinite page and screen variety, seems to us to be a sufficiently robust and inclusive principle for the brave new electronic world. 'Texts' would embrace the visual and the verbal, the spoken and the written, the literary and the non-literary, the local and the global. The pupil would be the producer of texts, as well as the collector and analyst of 'received' texts. The study of texts should protect against the dangers of prescription (the teaching of skills and drills at sentence and word levels); it should protect against elitism and nationalism (the teaching of an Anglocentric literary canon) and should give future teachers of English the confidence to reconfigure English teaching within the seamless spaces created by new technologies. Texts can provide the compass for a safe journey in such exciting territory. We wish you well.

NOTE

1 At the time of writing, Key Stage 3 Strategy training modules 'Assessment for Learning', incorporating Wiliam and Black's findings, are due for publication in spring 2004.

KEY TEXTS

Andrews, R. (2001) *Teaching and Learning English: A Guide to Recent Research and its Applications*. London: Continuum.

Department for Education and Skills (2002d) *Unlocking Potential: Raising Ethnic Minority Attainment at KS3*. London: DfES.

Mackey, M. (2002) *Literacies across Media: Playing the Text*. London: Routledge/Falmer.

Language Audit	Any Prior Knowledge	Degree or Other Professional Qualification	Professional Reading	Observation in Schools/College	Teaching in School/College	Experience and Knowledge during Training. Notes on Current Course Experience
Date and tick as appropriate:	e.g. 05/06/02					
Standards taken from NC for ITT in English						
Do you know and understand the principles of spoken and written - language as a system, including:						
LEXIS						
• **Morphology and semantics** – word structure, meanings and derivations						
• **Phonology** – the sound system of spoken words						
• **Graphology** – the alphabetic spelling system						
GRAMMATICAL						
• The **grammar** of spoken and written English, including:						
word classes and their functions in sentences						
word order and cohesion within sentences						
construction of complex sentences to include a variety of clauses and phrases						
co-ordination and subordination in sentences						
PUNCTUATION						
its relationship to the phrase and clause structure of sentences						
its use to denote emphasis						
conventions in writing						
TEXTUAL						
cohesion – the way that individual words, sentences and paragraphs work together to convey meaning, Including the logic and sequence of ideas						

Language Audit	Any Prior Knowledge	Degree or Other Professional Qualification	Professional Reading	Observation in Schools/College	Teaching in School/College	Experience and Knowledge during Training. Notes on Current Course Experience
organization, structure and presentation including the structure of written text						
Do you have a broad understanding of language as a social, cultural and historical phenomenon, including: historical changes in English, and its significance as a world language						
standard English and other dialects						
multilingualism and the learning of English as an additional language						
differences between spoken and written English						
Do you have knowledge about texts and critical approaches to them, including:						
analysis of different types of literary and non-literary texts, evaluating their quality and making judgements about them						
identification of the conventions associated with different types of text including non-fiction and media, and how they are used and changed for effect						
how information and ideas are presented, depencing on point of view, context, purpose and audience						
how to analyse texts for implication, undertone, bias, assertion, ambiguity						

APPENDIX 2

UNIT PLAN   LEARNING OBJECTIVES: CURRICULUM COVERAGE

Indicate clearly how you have drawn from relevant English documentation: Framework for KS3, NC 2000, GCSE or A level syllabus objectives, etc.
(Code for Framework reference: W1 = Word-Level Objective, Sn1 = Sentence-Level Objective. Ensure that one Key Objective is included in each unit plan. Indicate in bold.)

Ref. to Framework for English, NC2000, GCSE or A level objectives	Learning Objectives
	Speaking and Listening •
	Reading •
	Writing •

EXAMPLE

UNIT PLAN   LEARNING OBJECTIVES: CURRICULUM COVERAGE

Indicate clearly how you have drawn from relevant English documentation: Framework for KS3, NC 2000, GCSE or A level syllabus objectives, etc.

(Code for Framework reference: W1 = Word-Level Objective, Sn1 = Sentence-Level Objective. Ensure that one Key Objective is included in each unit plan. Indicate this in bold.)

Ref. to Framework for English, NC2000, GCSE or A level objectives	Learning Objectives: Year 9 Persuasive Writing
	Speaking and Listening
S&L 1	• reflect on the development of their abilities as speakers (in situations requiring persuasion)
S&L 6	• analyse bias in the spoken word eg.deliberate ambiguity, omission, abuse of evidence (see above)
S&L 7 **Key Objective**	• **Identify the underlying implications raised by a programme** (BBC Schools video)
	Reading
R 2 **Key Objective**	• **synthesise information from a range of sources, shaping material to meet the reader's needs**
R 4	• evaluate the relevance and reliability of information available in media sources
Sn11	• investigate current trends in language use
W6	• know and use terms that are useful for analysing language (of advertising)
	Writing
Wr 4	• choose, use and evaluate a range of presentational devices, on paper and on screen
Wr7	• explore how non-fiction texts can convey ideas or information in amusing or entertaining ways
Sn2	• use the full range of punctuation to emphasize meaning for a reader (in creating the advert)

'AT-A-GLANCE' UNIT PLAN

	WEEK 1	WEEK 2	WEEK 3	WEEK 4	Evolving/changing ideas
Content • • •	•	•	•	•	
Teaching and Learning Activities • • •	•	•	•	•	
Resources					
Assessment Points (might not be necessary each week)					

APPENDIX 5

ENGLISH LESSON PLAN   DATE:
TOPIC:

YEAR/ABILITY GROUP: DURATION:

LEARNING OBJECTIVES (refer to objectives in unit plan)
All pupils should be able to:

1.

2.

More able pupils should be able to:

1.

TEACHING AND LEARNING ACTIVITIES

Teaching Activity	Approx. Time	Learning Activity	Approx. Time

DIFFERENTIATED SUPPORT (e.g. your plans for SEN, EAL etc.):

ICT USE:

ASSESSMENT OPPORTUNITY:

HOMEWORK:

RESOURCES:

APPENDIX 6

EXAMPLE

YEAR/ABILITY GROUP: 9 (middle band)

DATE:

DURATION: 70 mins

LEARNING OBJECTIVES (refer to objectives in unit plan)

All pupils should be able to:

1. Present a point of view as persuasively as possible
2. Co-operate in pair and group oral work

More able pupils should be able to:

3. Be aware of the range of techniques used to persuade others, analysing the role of language

TEACHING AND LEARNING ACTIVITIES

Teaching Activity	Approx. Time	Learning Activity	Approx. Time
1.Teacher/pupil demonstration of A persuading B to do or think something	7 mins	2. Pupil A persuading Pupil B to do or think something.	8 mins
3. Whole class Feedback on (1 & 2) above			5 mins
		4. Groups of 4: spider diagrams on techniques of persuasion using internet & other media sources provided	15 mins
		5. Envoys: reps from each group move round and report back to own group	10 mins
6. Whole class: feedback on above			
7. Summary of what has been achieved and distribution of handout for homework			10 mins

DIFFERENTIATED SUPPORT (e.g. your plans for SEN, EAL etc.):

Mainly relying on differentiation of outcome: modelling at outset to help less confident. Teacher to select writing groups to ensure balance of ability

ICT USE:

Internet as a research tool producing 'handout' on successful communication to be used in next lesson

ASSESSMENT OPPORTUNITY:

Pair and group work will allow targeted teacher assessment of Speaking and Listening.

e.g. 'Contribute to and respond constructively in discussion, advocating and justifying a point of view.'

HOMEWORK:

Read Internet handout; collect range of examples of persuasive texts.

RESOURCES:

Marker pens; scheme of work; OHT + pupil copies; 'handout'.

APPENDIX 7

EVALUATION OF LESSON	
1. REVIEW OF LEARNING OBJECTIVES (Refer to your stated objectives)	
2. REVIEW OF TEACHING STRATEGIES (Refer to 2 or 3 TTA Standards only)	**Standard ref.**
3. TARGETS SET FOR NEXT LESSON	

Example:

EVALUATION OF LESSON	
1. REVIEW OF LEARNING OBJECTIVES **(Refer to your stated lesson objectives)** Paired activity was successful as example of social co-operation. They also discovered how difficult it was to persuade. Feedback here helped group activity, although they found this hard. I had to prompt them to think of ads., junk mail, politicians and techniques available. Feedback from group work suggested average and more able had got idea of repetitions, use of examples, humour. Envoy activity saved for next lesson – it should help lower ability (reinforcement) provided I do summary handout/OHT.	
2.REVIEW OF TEACHING STRATEGIES **(Refer to 2 or 3 TTA Standards)** Overestimated knowledge level for group work. They worked well enough to begin with but I recognized the signs of frustration and gave some whole class input to redirect them. A prompt sheet would have helped. Class is generally responsive but there is a broad spread of ability which I need to think carefully about when planning. Being very clear about my objectives and telling them at each stage of the lesson what they've achieved should help. The oral work gave me an opportunity to gauge their levels of confidence in Speaking and Listening. In future lessons I should be able to make assessment notes on one group per session.	**Standard ref.** 3.1.1 3.1.2 3.2
3. TARGETS SET FOR NEXT LESSON – produce a prompt sheet showing a range of techniques used 'to persuade' – ensure that I make my lesson objectives clear to them – check that I have enough very structured support material for lower ability children	

BIBLIOGRAPHY

Allen, N. (2002) 'Too much, too young? An analysis of the KS3 National Literacy Strategy in Practice', *English in Education*, 36 (1): 5–15.

Andrews, R. (2001) *Teaching and Learning English: A Guide to Recent Research and its Applications*. London: Continuum.

Barnes, D. (1992) 'The role of talk in learning', in K. Norman (ed.), *Thinking Voices: The Work of the National Oracy Project*. London: Hodder & Stoughton.

Beard, R. (2000) *Developing Writing 3–13*. London: Hodder & Stoughton.

Bearne, E. (ed.) (1999) *Use of Language across the Secondary Curriculum*. London: Routledge.

Beasley, P. (1994) *Hearsay: Performance Poetry Plus*. London: The Bodley Head.

Belsey, C. (1988) *Critical Practice*. London: Routledge.

Benton, M. and Fox, G. (1985) *Teaching Literature 9 to 14*. Oxford: Oxford University Press.

Berry, C. (1993) *The Actor and the Text*. London: Virgin Books.

Brereton, P. (2001) *The Continuum Guide to Media Education*. London: Continuum.

British Broadcasting Corporation (BBC) (1995) *Pride and Prejudice*. London: BBC Publications.

British Film Institute (BFI) (1991) *Secondary Media Education: A Curriculum Statement*. London: BFI.

Brumfit, C. (1995) *Language Education in the National Curriculum*. Oxford: Blackwell.

Buckingham, D. (ed.) (1990) *Watching Media Learning: Making Sense of Media Education*. London: Falmer Press.

Buckingham, D. (2000) *After the Death of Childhood: Growing up in the Age of Electronic Media*. Cambridge: Polity Press.

Buckingham, D. and Sefton-Green, J. (1994) *Cultural Studies Goes to School: Reading and Teaching Popular Culture*. London: Taylor & Francis.

Bunyan, P. et al. (2000) *Cracking Drama: Progression in Drama within English (5–16)*. Sheffield: NATE.

Burton, M. (ed.) (1989) *Enjoying Texts: Using Literary Theory in the Classroom*. Cheltenham: Stanley Thornes.

Cameron, D. (1995) *Verbal Hygiene*. London: Routledge.

Carter, R. (ed.) (1990) *Knowledge about Language and the National Curriculum: The LINC Reader*. London: Hodder & Stoughton.

Carter, R. (1995) *Keywords in Language and Literacy*. London: Routledge.

Carter, R. (1997) *Investigating English Discourse: Language, Literacy and Literature*. London: Routledge.

Clipson-Boyles, S. (1998) 'Developing oracy through drama', in J. Holderness and B. Lalljee (eds), *An Introduction to Oracy: Frameworks for Talk*. London: Cassell.

Cox, B. (1991) *Cox on Cox: An English Curriculum for the 1990s*. London: Hodder & Stoughton.

Cox, B. (1995) *Cox on the Battle for the English Curriculum*. London: Hodder & Stoughton.

Crystal, D. (1996) *Rediscover Grammar*. Harlow: Longman.

Crystal, D. (1997) *The Cambridge Encyclopedia of Language* (2nd edn). Cambridge:

Cambridge University Press.

D'Arcy, P. (2000) *Two Contrasting Paradigms for the Teaching and Assessment of Writing.* Sheffield: NATE.

Daly, C. (2000) 'Gender differences in achievement', in J. Davison and J. Moss (eds), *Issues in English Teaching.* London: Routledge.

Davies, C. (1996) *What is English Teaching?* Buckingham: Open University Press.

Davison J. and Moss J. (eds) (2000) *Issues in English Teaching.* London: Routledge.

Day, B (2001a) *Mixed Media: Teacher's Book.* Oxford: Oxford University Press.

Day, B. (2001b) *Mixed Media: Pupils' Book.* Oxford: Oxford University Press.

Dean, G. (2000) *Teaching Reading in Secondary Schools.* London: David Fulton.

Department for Education and Employment (DfEE) (1998) *The National Literacy Strategy: Framework for Teaching.* Sudbury: DfEE Publications.

Department for Education and Employment (DfEE) (1999) *English: The National Curriculum for English.* London: DfEE/QCA.

Department for Education and Employment (DfEE) (2000) *The National Literacy Strategy: Grammar for Writing.* London, DfEE.

Department for Education and Employment (DfEE) (2001a) *Literacy across the Curriculum.* Sudbury: DfEE Publications.

Department for Education and Employment (DfEE) (2001b) *Framework for Teaching English: Years 7, 8 and 9.* Sudbury: DfEE Publications.

Department for Education and Employment (DfEE) (2001c) *English Department Training 2001.* Sudbury: DfEE Publications.

Department for Education and Employment (DfEE) (2001d) *Year 7 Speaking and Listening Bank.* Sudbury: DfEE Publications.

Department for Education and Employment (DfEE) (2001e) *Developing Early Writing.* London: DfEE.

Department for Education and Skills (DfES) (2002a) *Training Materials for the Foundation Subjects.* London: DfES.

Department for Education and Skills (DfES) (2002b) *Grammar for Writing: Supporting Pupils Learning EAL.* Sudbury: DfES Publications.

Department for Education and Skills (DfES) (2002c) *English Department Training 2002/3 Year 8 Course Tutor's Notes.* Sudbury: DfES Publications.

Department for Education and Skills (DfES) (2002d) *Unlocking Potential: Raising Ethnic Minority Attainment at KS3.* London: DfES.

Department of Education and Science (DES) (1989) *English for Ages 5 to 16* (Cox Report). London: HMSO.

Dias, P. and Hayhoe M. (1988) *Developing Response to Poetry.* Buckingham: Open University Press.

Duffy, C.A. (1999) *The World's Wife.* London: Picador.

Eagleton, T. (1996) *Literary theory: An Introduction* (2nd edn). Oxford: Blackwell.

Fairclough, N. (1992) *Critical Language Awareness.* Harlow: Longman.

Fairclough, N. (2001) *Language and Power* (2nd edn). Harlow: Longman.

Frater, G. (2001) *Effective Practice in Writing at KS2* . London: Basic Skills Agency. .

Gardner, H. (1993) *Frames of Mind: The Theory of Multiple Intelligences.* London: Fontana Press.

Gibson, R. (1998) *Teaching Shakespeare.* Cambridge: Cambridge University Press.

Gibson, R. (ed.) (1995) *The Tempest.* Cambridge: Cambridge University Press.

Goleman, D. (1996) *Emotional Intelligence: Why it Can Matter More than IQ.* London: Bloomsbury.

Goodwyn, A. (1992) *English Teaching and Media Education.* Buckingham: Open University Press.

Goodwyn, A. (ed.) (1998) *Literary and Media Texts in Secondary English: New Approaches.* London: Cassell.

Goodwyn, A. (1999) 'The Cox models revisited: English teachers' views of their subject and the National Curriculum', *English in Education*, 33 (2): 19–31.

Goodwyn, A. (ed.) (2000) *English in the Digital Age*. London: Cassell.

Graddol, D. (2001) 'English in the Future', in A. Burns and C. Coffin (eds), *Analysing English in a Global Context*. London: Routledge.

Grainger, T. (2002) 'Drama and writing: passion on the page', *The Secondary English Magazine*, 5 (2).

Griffiths, P. (1997) *Introducing Media: Newspapers, Advertising, Television, Radio and Film*. Harlow: Longman.

Hall, N. (1999) 'Young children, play and literacy', in J. Marsh and E. Hallet (eds), *Desirable Literacies: Approaches to Language and Literacy in the Early Years*. London: Paul Chapman Publishing.

Hall, N. and Robinson, A. (1995) *Exploring Writing and Play in the Early Years*. London : David Fulton.

Haworth, A. (2002) 'Literacy tests for trainee teachers: shadows across the secondary classroom?', *Cambridge Journal of Education*, 32 (3): 289–302.

Heathcote, D. and Wagner, B. (1999) *Drama as a Learning Medium*. Portland, ME: Calendar Islands.

Hilton, M. (2003) 'Media literacies: a review', *English in Education*, 37 (1): 60–1.

Holliday, A. (2000) 'Exploring other worlds: escaping linguistic parochialism', in J. Davison and J. Moss (eds), *Issues in English Teaching*. London: Routledge.

Hornbrook, D. (ed.) (1998) *On the Subject of Drama*. London: Routledge.

Hunt, P. (1991) *Criticism, Theory, and Children's Literature*. Oxford: Blackwell.

Kearney, C. (2000) 'Eyes wide shut: recent educational policy in the light of changing notions of English identity', *English in Education*, 34 (3): 19–30.

Keith, G. (1994) *Get the Grammar*. London: BBC Publications.

Keith, G. (1997) 'Teach yourself English grammar', *English & Media Magazine*, 36: 8–12.

Keith, G. and Shuttleworth, J. (1997) *Living Language: Exploring Advanced Level English Language*. London: Hodder & Stoughton.

King, P. (2002) 'Does the model of English in the National Literacy Strategy create failure for pupils from differing language backgrounds?', *English in Education*, 36 (2): 7–17.

Kitchen, D. (1988) *Earshot: A Poetry Anthology*. London: Heinemann.

Kress, G. (1995) *Writing the Future: English and the Making of a Culture of Innovation*. Sheffield: NATE.

Leask, M. and Pachler, N. (1999) *Learning to Teach Using ICT in the Secondary School*. London: Routledge.

Lewis, M. and Wray, D. (1997) *Writing Frames: Scaffolding Children's Non-fiction Writing in a Range of Genres*. Reading: Reading and Language Information Centre.

Lunzer, E. and Gardner, K. (1979) *The Effective Use of Reading*. London: Heinemann.

Mackey, M. (2002) *Literacies across Media: Playing the Text*. London: Routledge/Falmer.

Marsh, J. and Millard, E. (2000) *Literacy and Popular Culture: Using Children's Culture in the Classroom*. London: Paul Chapman Publishing.

Marshall, B. (2000) *English Teachers: The Unofficial Guide: Researching the Philosophies of English*. London: Routledge.

Masterman, L. (1985) *Teaching the Media*. London: Comedia.

Maybin, J. (2000) 'The Canon: historical construction and contemporary challenges', in J. Davison and J. Moss (eds), *Issues in English Teaching*. London: Routledge.

Meek, M. (1991) *On Being Literate*. London: The Bodley Head.

Mercer, N. (1995) *The Guided Construction of Knowledge: Talk Amongst Teachers & Learners*. Clevedon: Multilingual Matters.

Millard, E. (1994) *Developing Readers in the Middle Years* (2nd edn). Buckingham: Open University Press.

Millard, E. (2000) *Differently Literate: Boys, Girls and the Schooling of Literacy*. London: Falmer.

Myhill, D (2001) *Better Writers*. Suffolk: Courseware Publications.

National Association for the Teaching of English (NATE) (1998) *Drama* (Position Paper). Sheffield: NATE.

National Advisory Committee on Creative and Cultural Education (NACCCE) (1999) *All Our Futures: Creativity, Culture and Education*. Sudbury: DfEE Publications.

National Oracy Project (NOP) (1991) *Teaching Talking and Learning in Key Stage 3*. York: National Curriculum Council.

Neelands, J. (1992) *Learning Through Imagined Experience: The Role of Drama in the National Curriculum*. London: Hodder & Stoughton.

Neelands, J. (1998) *Beginning Drama 11–14*. London: David Fulton.

Neelands, J. (2000) *Structuring Drama Work*. Cambridge: Cambridge University Press.

Norman, K. (ed.) (1992) *Thinking Voices: The Work of the National Oracy Project*. London: Hodder & Stoughton.

Peim, N. (1993) *Critical Theory and the English Teacher: Transforming the Subject*. London: Routledge.

Perera, K. (1984) *Children's Writing and Reading*. Oxford: Blackwell.

Qualifications and Curriculum Authority (1998) *The Grammar Papers: Perspectives on the Teaching of Grammar in the National Curriculum*. London: QCA.

Qualifications and Curriculum Authority (QCA) (1999a) *Not Whether but How: Teaching Grammar at Key Stages 3 and 4*. London: QCA.

Qualifications and Curriculum Authority (QCA) (1999b) *Improving Writing at Key Stages 3 and 4*. London: QCA.

Race, P. (1993) *Never Mind the Teaching, Feel the Learning* (SEDA paper 80). Birmingham: SEDA.

Sage, R. (2000) *Class Talk: Successful Learning through Effective Communication*. Stafford: Network Educational Press.

Scher, A. and Verrall, C. (1976) *100+ Ideas for Drama*. London: Heinemann.

Slade, P. (1954) *Child Drama*. London: University of London Press.

Smith, F. and Hardman, F. (2000) 'Evaluating the effectiveness of the National Literacy Strategy: identifying the indicators of success', *Educational Studies*, 26 (3): 365–78.

Snyder, I. (ed.) (1998) *Page to Screen: Taking Literacy into the Electronic Era*. London: Routledge.

Snyder, I., Angus, L. and Sutherland-Smith, W. (2002) 'Building equitable literate futures: home and school computer-mediated literacy practices and disadvantage', *Cambridge Journal of Education*, 32 (3): 367–83.

Stubbs, M. (1990) *Knowledge about Language: Grammar, Ignorance and Society*. London: Institute of Education, London University.

Tannen, D. (ed.) (1986) *Spoken & Written Language*. Norwood, NJ: Ablex.

Teacher Training Agency (TTA) (2000) *Raising the Attainment of Minority Ethnic Pupils*. London: TTA.

Wiliam, D. and Black, P. (1998) *Inside the Black Box: Raising Standards through Classroom Assessment*. London: School of Education, King's College London.

Wiliam, D. and Black, P. (2002) 'Feedback is the best nourishment', *TES Extra*, 4 October.

Wiliam, D. and Black, P. (2002) *Working Inside the Black Box*. London: Department of Education and Professional Studies, King's College London.

Wilkinson, A. (1965) 'A test of listening comprehension', *Educational Review*, 18 (3): 177–85.

Wilkinson, A. (1968) 'The implications of oracy', *Educational Review*, 20 (2): 123–35.

Wray, D. and Lewis M. (1997) *Extending Literacy: Children Reading and Writing Non-fiction*. London: Routledge.

Wrigley, S. (2003) 'More testing times for literacy', *NATE News*, January, no. 21: 1–4.

Index

Accent, 96
assessment, 136–8, 157–9
  criteria, 99
  of drama, 116–117
  formative, 97
  GCSE, 117
  summative, 112
  of writing, 62–4
Audit of subject knowledge,
    Appendix 1, 100

beginner writers, 55
British Film Institute, 129, 136–7
Brumfit, C., 14

Carter, R., 24, 46–7
Citizenship, 90
cohesion, 37, 46
communication, 142
critical discourse analysis, 13, 24–5
cultural studies, 125, 157
culture, 126

Dialect, 96
digital video editing, 148–9
discourse grammar, 46
Drama, 97, 98, 100
  in English, 102–122
  hot seat, 110, 115
  improvisation, 103, 109, 115
  management, 112–114
  mime, 115, 119, 120
  planning, 112–114

role-play, 103, 115
techniques, 115–116

electronic dictionary, 143
English
  models, 73
  as perceived by teachers, 2–3
  spoken & written, 30
  subject history, 1
  varieties of academic English,
    1–2
English as an Additional Language
    [EAL], 27–8, 47, 107
English for ages 5–16, 29
Evaluation, 100
  peer, 99

*Framework for Teaching English: years
    7, 8 and 9*, 18, 39, 43, 47,
    51–53, 156–7
  key objectives, 39
  word-, sentence-, text-level
    objectives, 18, 44, 53
  see also Objectives
future of English, 155–160

GCSE English, 96, 100
  assessment, 117
  coursework, 97, 98
  drama, 104
genre, 22, 25, 40, 52–4
grammar, 16, 30, 35–48
  in action, 46

classroom applications, 40–1,
44–5
and cognition, 38–9, 46–7
definitions of, 37
and English as an Additional
Language [EAL], 47
map of, 42–3
of Media language, 131
models of teaching, 37–9, 42–3,
46,
and the National Curriculum,
39–40, 42–3
and power, 39, 41
sentence-level, 37–8
terminology, 18–20, 36–8, 40,
42–3, 46
and writing, 30, 38–9, 46–7
Grammar for Writing, 47, 57–8

ICT, 133, 155–7
*Improving Writing at key stages 3 &
4*, 37, 46, 58
inclusion, 159–160
Initial Teacher Training, 94
internet, 141, 144

Keith, G., 38, 42–4
Key Stage 3 Strategy, 14, 49, 52, 58,
60, 94, 104, 105
see also the National Strategy, the
Strategy
knowledge about language, 16
implicit/explicit
see also Language
Kroll, B.M., 55

language, 12–33
audit, 18–20, 161–2
charter, 14
classroom applications, 20–3,
27–28
explicit/implicit knowledge of, 16

see also knowledge
functional theories of, 24
and literacy, 31–4
models of, 23–5
and the national curriculum,
16–18, 26, 28, 31–3
and power, 3–14, 18, 28, 41
study, 16, 18, 20–5, 37
variation, 18, 25–31
and whole school issues, 14–15
Learning
and objectives, 116
and pedagogy, 11
lesson plans, 31–4, 44–5, 60–1
see also planning
Liberal Humanist Tradition, 126
LINC project, 23–4, 37–8
linguistic terminology, 18–19,
23–5, 36
see *also* grammar
literacy[ies], 14–15, 103
across the curriculum, 14–15,
46, 53
hour, 52
multimedia, 156–7
new arrival, 6–7
support materials, 46
literary canon, 126
literature
and civilizing values, 74
connecting literary critical theory
and pedagogy, 79
and culture, heritage, national
identity, 80
demystifying literary texts, 123,
129
and literary critical theory, 75
and reader-response theory, 75
and speaking and listening, 86–7
and writing, 87–8

Mackey, M., 156

multilingualism, 27–8
Mindmapping, 96
Myhill, D., 38, 57

National Association for the
    teaching of English [NATE], 158
National Curriculum for English,
    37, 44, 53, 55, 58–60, 90, 91,
    102, 104, 105, 107, 118, 156
    assessment, 159–60
    attainment targets, 18, 20–2, 26,
National Literacy Strategy [NLS,
    primary], 18, 39–40, 42–3,
    51–3, 58, 104, 105, 118
    Plenary, 107
National Oracy Project, 91
National Strategy, 14, 49, 52, 58,
    60, 92
    see also Key Stage 3 Strategy, the
        Strategy

objectives, 18, 156
    key, 39
    word-, sentence-, text-level
        objectives, 18, 44
    see also Framework
objectives-led learning, 158
OFSTED, 104
Oracy, 90–101
    assessment, 96–97

Perera, K., 55–6
planning, 31–4, 44–5, 60–1
    see also lesson planning
Plenary, 107
Progression, 96
    in drama, 116–117

Qualifications and Curriculum
    Authority [QCA], xiv, 38, 46, 58

radio, 130–1, 151–2
reading
    elements, 66, 68–9
    progress, 66–7, 69–72
    skimming and scanning, 144

Shakespeare, 117–122
simulation
    computer generated, 147, 150–3
soap opera, 126–7, 131, 134–5
Special Educational Needs, 106,
    107
spoken/written English, 30–1, 47
standard English, 5, 18, 29–30,
    30–1
    spoken 92, 93, 96
    written, 92
standards
    complaints tradition, 5–6
    raising, 7
    rising, 8
the Strategy, 14, 49, 52, 58, 60
    see also Key Stage 3 Strategy,
        national strategy

technology, 133, 139, 141
testing, 158
text[s] 24–5, 36, 38, 44, 48, 53–4,
    56, 160
    constructedness, 78
    definition, x
    ICT and digital texts, 142–3, 147
    media texts, 129–130
    and value judgements, 80
    variety and range, 4, 9–10, 77–8
Trainee teachers, 31, 44, 93, 94, 95

Units of study, 94, 101

visual literacy, 131–2

Wiliam & Black, 63–4, 158–160
word processor, 145–7, 148
writing, 49–64
   assessment of, 62–4
   classroom applications, 59, 60–1
   conditions for, 50–4
   development of, 54–6
   extended, 51
   frames, 52–3
   genres, 53
   guided, 53–4
   instructional/informational, 60–1
   message/mechanics, 57–8
   and the National Curriculum, 53, 58–9
   shared, 53–4
   and thinking, 56
written/spoken English, 30–1, 54–5